PASTOR'S WIFE SURVIVAL PLAYBOOK

A Thriving Marriage & Ministry in the Mayhem

TERRY AND KELLY THOMPSON

Copyright Page Information:

Pastor's Wife Survival Playbook: A Thriving Marriage & Ministry in the Mayhem

ISBN 978-1-948022-21-7

Rainer Publishing
www.RainerPublishing.com
Spring Hill, TN

Printed in the United States of America

DEDICATION

This book is dedicated to the unsung heroes of pastoral ministry, the pastor's wives. The old saying is, "behind every good man there is a good woman". We believe this statement to be true, as do the pastors who have a faithful wife at their side. Thank you for loving Jesus, loving the church, standing by your man, caring for your family, and ministering to others. May God richly bless your faithfulness.

ACKNOWLEDGEMENTS

A sincere and heartfelt thanks to:

- Our wonderful daughters and sons-in-law – Katie and Caleb and Holly and Brad. Thank you for loving us so well. Thank you for giving us grandchildren. Thank you for all the sermon illustrations.
- Our parents – Dave and Carol and Frank and Della. Thank you for never questioning our call to full time ministry. You have always been our prayer warriors and cheerleaders.
- Our Rock Point Church family – you have made pastoral ministry a joy and a blessing. Our family forever. Thank you!
- To those who patiently helped us learn how to write and publish a book. Rex Ryker, Brian Croft, Carol Thompson, Becki Brueggeman, PJ Croy and Sam Rainer. Thank you!
- To the Covid-19 shutdown, which provided us the bandwidth to write this book. A silver lining to a very dark cloud.

CONTENTS

INTRODUCTION

Why This Book?

Hi, I'm Kelly. I have been a pastor's wife since 1985. When my pastor-husband Terry and I started a ministry called Small Church USA, he thought it would be a good idea for us to write a book from my perspective as a pastor's wife, since pastor's wives are one of the focal points of our ministry. Now, here is what you need to know about my husband. He is a creative visionary and usually has big ministry ideas floating around in his head. Every now and then he will drop an idea on me to get my thoughts and reactions. Over the years I have always been a willing participant as his sounding board and a voice of reason, but it was different when this idea came floating out. This idea directly involved me; and trust me, it was so far outside my box that I couldn't even see my box. So, after much prayer, here is how it went down. I was reluctant. We negotiated. I said yes. And he agreed to flesh out the final thoughts on paper. It didn't cause us to end up in marriage counseling, so that was a big win. Honestly, it has been an enjoyable journey as we have collaborated on this project together. Go team.

Living in Small-Town America

In case you are wondering if I can relate to your ministry situation, here's mine. The first fourteen years of our ministry we lived in Indianapolis, Indiana, and Columbus, Ohio. They were developing and growing years for us as we learned about "church world" in large metropolitan settings. In 1998 God gave us a new assignment and we moved to spacious west central Indiana and put down roots in what is now our home community of Crawfordsville. It's small-town America at its finest, and yes, as we would discover, it's a completely different animal than big-city living.

With a population of 15,000 people, Crawfordsville is surrounded by agricultural fields with livestock a common sight when taking a scenic drive through the countryside. The nearest city is a forty-mile drive, so if a stop is needed at Target, Sam's Club, or Hobby Lobby, it gets included on the date night agenda. Thankfully, we do have a local Walmart and, after living here for twenty-two years, a Starbucks just opened. Hallelujah! Miracles still happen!

According to the U.S. Census Bureau, 91 percent of all the communities in the United States of America have a population of 15,000 people or less, just like Crawfordsville. This would indicate there are thousands of churches, pastors, and pastors' wives ministering in communities just like ours. If you're looking to connect with a pastor's wife who understands the dynamics of a big city or a small town and who can relate to your ministry experiences, I just might be the person. Let's do this journey together.

Breaking the Ice with Transparency

Big breath (that's for me, not you), and here we go. My goal in this project is to be a refreshing and encouraging voice to pastors' wives. Being the wife of a pastor is one of those unique positions that you only understand if you are in it. Since I have held that unique title since day one of our marriage, I guess I am qualified to write this book. But from the standpoint of having all the answers, or doing it all right, or having it all figured out, I am potentially the least qualified. If you're looking for a book from the "I have it all together" pastor's wife, you have chosen the wrong book.

Trust me, there is nothing extraordinary about me. I am a small-town girl from Michigan. My parents both worked at General Motors. When I was young, they both accepted Christ and began taking me to church. Our church was small, conservative, and legalistic. My four older brothers turned me into a tomboy at an early age, as I often thought my life was in peril from their antics. I attended a small Christian school then moved away from home and attended a small Bible college before getting married and heading into ministry. I hold an elementary education teaching degree and taught school for several years. When we moved to Crawfordsville, Terry became the lead pastor of a church of twenty people, in desperate need of revitalization, and I became his volunteer secretary. Over the next twenty-plus years as the church grew to over 1,000 people, I transitioned into being the office manager. I am a mom of two wonderful girls and Grammy to several energetic grandkids. I love Jesus, our family, sports, Young Living essential oils, traveling and ministry . . . and let's not forget, Hallmark Christmas movies.

Oh, and then there are my flaws. We might as well address these right from the get-go. Let's see; I am a people pleaser, I have the spiritual gift of sarcasm, I fear failure, I have some trauma from my early years, my marriage isn't perfect, my kids aren't perfect, our church isn't perfect, and I may have an addiction issue with good coffee. Yes, I am much like all the other pastors' wives in this world. I do life and ministry one day at a time. Some days are good, and others are extremely challenging. I have discovered over the years that being married to a pastor and trying to figure out ministry is like trying to hit a moving target. I readily admit that shooting at a moving target means you often miss the mark. So if you're okay with an ordinary pastor's wife being humbly honest, transparent, and real, then I'm good to give this a go. May God shower us with his abundant grace as we strive together to be pastors' wives who please Christ and add value to our husbands' ministries.

Middle School and Dodgeball

When we look back on life, we often discover that we learn some valuable lessons in odd places. Take middle school, for example. Talk about an odd and clumsy time in our adolescent years. For us girls these years were challenging at best. We faced a giant learning curve as we moved from being children into being teenagers. Hormones seemingly turned little girls into all kinds of interesting creatures. As we walked through the front doors of middle school for the first time, it was evident that things had changed. In a matter of a few short months there were all kinds of new issues in our lives: peer pressure, social pecking order, body image, cool kids, non-cool kids, athletic-team cuts, opening a locker, changing classrooms, hair styles, clothing fashions, co-ed parties, boys, and yes, gym class.

Looking back at my middle school years, it was in gym class where I learned some valuable lessons about life and about being a pastor's wife. You see, back in the day, gym class had few rules about being nice; it was more of a gladiator philosophy: "full contact sports will toughen you up and make you stronger." It was win or lose; no trophies awarded for participation. Hence, the game of dodgeball was invented. It was easy to figure out dodgeball day. The class began with all the boys lined up in a single-file line and all the girls doing the same in their own line. Then the count off started, 1 . . . 2 . . . 1 . . . 2 . . . 1 . . . 2. All the boys and girls who counted off as 1's went to one end of the gym, all the 2's to the other end. The teacher would announce it was dodgeball day and then proceed to explain the three simple rules.

1. If you get hit, you're out.
2. If you hit someone in the head, you're out, and they are still in.
3. If someone catches your ball, you're out, and a person from the other team comes back in.

Then the teacher would place six rubber kick balls on the center line of the gym floor, make everyone line up against the end walls, blow the whistle, and then all sorts of chaos and mayhem would break loose for the next thirty minutes.

In the end, some win, some lose, some laugh through the pain while others cry, some enjoy it, some hate it, some embrace and strategize, some give up quickly, some want to quit and never play it again while others want to play it every day. Good old middle school PE class. What a crazy season of life.

Here are five life lessons that I call "pastor-wife training 101" from middle school dodgeball.

1. Life and ministry will at times be chaos and mayhem.
2. There will be great wins and painful losses.
3. People, including you and those you love, will get hurt.
4. Some will give up and quit.
5. Some will embrace the chaos.

The fifth lesson I learned from junior high dodge ball was the most important. In life and ministry, the key to not simply survive but thrive is to embrace and strategize in the midst of the chaos and mayhem.

Chaos is defined as "complete disorder and confusion."

Mayhem is defined as "violent or damaging disorder."

Yes, that pretty much describes my recollection of a middle school dodge ball game as well as life and ministry.

Help! I Married a Pastor!

I became a pastor's wife in 1985. I had no clue. I had no help. I had no Bible college classes. I had no books. I had no strategy. I had no mentor. It was like entering a dodgeball game blindfolded. Can you even imagine? Who in their right mind would put on a blindfold before entering a dodge ball game? In our youth ministry days, we used to turn off all the lights in the church gym and play strobe light dodgeball with the teens. That was crazy and chaotic for sure, not to mention an instant headache. But never did we entertain the thought of playing blindfolded. That would not just be crazy; that would be insane.

Looking back at starting ministry as a young pastor's wife, with no playbook at all, now seems like a bit of insanity. In those early years when the balls of life started whizzing past my head from all different directions, I wasn't always sure what to do. Do I attack? Do I run? Do I hide in the corner? Do I cry? Do I give up and quit? Do I hold my ground? I was a twenty-two-year-old, newlywed bride, right out of college. I had just married the love of my life who was called to be a pastor. To be honest, there were many times I felt like I was in the dark and completely overwhelmed. And from the many pastors' wives I have talked to over the years, this seems to be a common storyline.

A Sneak Peek

My prayer is that this short book will be an encouragement to pastors' wives who find themselves in the middle of the dodgeball game of life and ministry. For our husbands there is a biblical manual, job description and qualifications clearly spelled out in God's Word for their duties and responsibilities. For pastors' wives, there is no such clarity. I hope to share a few principles from God's Word and a few practices from years of ministry life that might be helpful in attempting to remove the blindfold.

We will take a brief look at seven realities of ministry life I believe pastors wives need to manage, deal with, and strategize through in order to survive and thrive in the chaos and mayhem. Here is a brief outline:

A pastor's wife needs to manage, deal with and strategize through the reality of:

Chapter 1: HIS Calling
Chapter 2: My Assignment
Chapter 3: His Good
Chapter 4: Their Expectations
Chapter 5: His Battles
Chapter 6: Our Discouragements
Chapter 7: Our Family

Each chapter will be broken down into four specific sections.

- The Dodgeball Warriors
- The Woman of the Word
- The Real-Life Ministry World
- The Questions to Wrestle

An Unexpected Beginning

Do you remember your first actual days of ministry? You drive the loaded U-Haul into an unfamiliar and unknown town. You unpack and settle into your new apartment. Then there is the first Sunday. As you pull into the parking lot your stomach feels as if it is filled with butterflies. The anticipation of getting started has finally arrived. As you walk in the front doors you can sense that everyone's eyes are on you. People are friendly and excited to have you on the team, but your brain is immediately on overload. There are so many things to process: Will I remember people's names?

Will I fit in? What is the culture of the church really like? Will the teens like me as much as they did the last youth pastors' wife? The day ends up being great but a bit of a blur. This ministry is what you have been preparing for all through Bible college, and it is finally coming to fruition. Oh, the excitement and energy! Do you remember?

Yes, that is how I felt. I was energized and ready to dive in headfirst. Then this happened. And yes, this really did happen! During one of our first few days on the job the lead pastor of our new church and his wife invited us over to their home for dinner. The thought was much appreciated, and we enjoyed a nice meal and conversation. Then, as the evening went along, the unexpected happened. The pastor's wife decided to share a confidence with me. Now, I would think that is a little unusual given the circumstances. But then what she shared with me, I will never forget. The sentence was only six-words, "I hate being a pastor's wife!" Now, that was a deer-in-the-headlights moment for me. What was I to say to that? How should I respond? It's one of those moments when a thousand things go through your mind in an instant. Why would she say that to me? Why did she feel that way? What would cause such pain and hurt? I was counting on her to be my mentor. What would that relationship look like now? I was speechless. I was in shock. I hardly even knew this lady. It was an awkward moment to say the least, and her statement ended without me giving a reply. I had no words.

Later that evening, as the shock factor went away and my head cleared, I began to wonder. If years of being a pastor's wife brought her to this place of discouragement and defeat, what would years of ministry do to me? After Terry and I had been at this for a length of time, would I also hate being a pastor's wife? I will never forget that evening and the statement, "I hate being a pastor's wife." As the old saying goes, "You never get a second chance to make a first impression." Her statement made an impression all right. It is a conversation I vividly remember yet to this day.

Please understand, I do not share that story to throw stones or cast judgment. I had no idea about her ministry background or experiences. I had not walked in her shoes. As a newlywed bride, literally in her first few days of ministry, I knew nothing of the challenges of being a pastor's wife or what might lie ahead for me, therefore I refused to condemn. Far too many times we fall into the trap of drawing conclusions before understanding the full context of a person's story. We would be wise to exercise discernment and listen carefully before placing blame. God's Word reminds us that jumping to conclusions is a foolish and prideful way to live.

> To answer before listening— that is folly and shame. (Proverbs 18:13)

> Do not judge, or you too will be judged. For in the same way you judge others, you will be judged, and with the measure you use, it will be measured to you. Why do you look at the

> speck of sawdust in your brother's eye and pay no attention to the plank in your own eye? How can you say to your brother, "Let me take the speck out of your eye,' when all the time there is a plank in your own eye? You hypocrite, first take the plank out of your own eye, and then you will see clearly to remove the speck from your brother's eye." (Matthew 7:1–5)

What I can now perceive is this: sadly, somewhere along the way, her journey had been one of disappointment and pain. Still to this day my heart is heavy as I think back to that evening and this hurting lady. Today, that conversation also causes me to wonder how many pastors' wives, if they were honest, might say the same thing: "I hate being a pastors' wife."

Not Alone on an Island

By God's grace, I am so thankful as I look back over the years of being a pastor's wife that my experience has not been hers. I love being a pastor's wife—well, at least most days—and I believe there are some reasons why. It is my prayer that this book will provide some practical tools that will help create a ministry pathway that is a blessing and not a burden. Let me encourage you with this reality as we begin: you are not alone in your calling as a pastor's wife. Trust me; you are not on an island. There are literally thousands of us on the same island needing the essential, life-giving hope found in God's Word that encourages us to love and support one another. The apostle Paul's words to the church at Thessalonica easily apply to all believers, and yes, to pastors' wives as well.

> Therefore, encourage one another and build each other up, just as in fact you are doing. (1 Thessalonians 5:11)

Isolation is dangerous; so let's find each other, lock arms, reach out, pray and embrace this calling, it will be of benefit to all.

Ready or not, I just heard the whistle blow. We are in the game; take off the blindfold, because here come the balls! And yes, they are coming hard and fast!

On a side note, as I mentioned earlier, I grew up with four older brothers. Talk about mayhem and chaos! And yes, I loved gym class and dodgeball. Thanks for all the training Mark, Tony, Bud, and Mike.

The Questions to Wrestle

1. As you think about middle school dodgeball, or just middle school in general, what do you remember? Is it a good or painful memory?
2. Kelly was open and transparent about her flaws right from the start. Share a couple of your "flaws" that are challenging to you in your life and ministry.
3. What do you think of the five life lessons for ministry? Have you found those to be true? Share a few examples.
4. Were you equipped for ministry, or did you go into it blindfolded? What are some of the areas you feel you had to face blindfolded?
5. It is heartbreaking to hear a woman say, "I hate being a pastor's wife." Have you ever been there? If yes, are you still there? If no, how do you keep from getting there?

CHAPTER 1

HIS CALLING

The Dodgeball Warriors—"Drafted"

In many arenas of life we get "drafted," as it were, and there isn't an option as to whether or not to participate. Like it or not, we are in the game! Areas like the family we were born into, attending school, doing chores, taking gym class, and yes, playing dodgeball should have taught us that important life lesson. There was never an option to "sit this one out" on dodgeball day. The decision to join the chaos was already made by someone else. So, since we were "drafted" to play, we had two choices: hide in the corner and wait to take a painful elimination shot and sit on the sidelines, or actively join the team, embrace the chaos and mayhem, and help fight for the win.

I think we would all acknowledge that life is a series of events, many of which we cannot control, and then a corresponding series of choices. Our choices boil down to two simple options: we can choose to be the victim or the game changer. I believe God called pastors' wives to change the game.

I'm reminded of an obscure woman in the Bible named Jael. She was a game changer. During the reign of Deborah, in the time of the judges, there was a fierce battle between Israel and the powerful Canaanites living in Hazor. Jael secured the victory for the Israelites by killing the captain of the Canaanite armies. Her feat of bravery was so heroic that Deborah wrote a song about that victory and how Jael changed the game.

> Most blessed of women be Jael, the wife of Heber the Kenite, most blessed of tent-dwelling women. He asked for water, and she gave him milk; in a bowl fit for nobles she brought him curdled milk. Her hand reached for the tent peg, her right hand for the workman's hammer. She struck Sisera, she crushed his head, she shattered and pierced his temple. At her feet he sank, he fell; there he lay. At her feet he sank, he fell; where he sank, there he fell—dead. (Judges 5:24–27)

It would have been easy for this nomadic, tent-dwelling woman to sit on the sidelines and let others engage in the battle. No one would have blamed her for making that decision or taking that role. But instead of being a bystander, she engaged in the game and assisted in bringing home the victory.

There is another game-changing woman mentioned in 2 Samuel. Her name is never given, she is simply referred to as "a wise woman." As King David's soldiers are pursuing an enemy commander, he hides within the city walls of Abel Beth-Maakah. Joab, the leader of David's army, and his men build a siege ramp and begin battering the city walls in order to enter the city. Had they broken through, it would have been catastrophic for the people who lived there. One person decided to be a difference maker. This no-name wise woman decides not to be a victim and sit on the sidelines. In a bold move, she requests a conversation with Joab. In their meeting he agrees to spare the city if they hand over the enemy commander, Sheba. She talks to the city leaders, and they hand over the commander, thus sparing the entire city. Here is how God's Word records the details of this event.

> Sheba passed through all the tribes of Israel to Abel Beth-Maakah and through the entire region of the Bikrites, who gathered together and followed him. All the troops with Joab came and besieged Sheba in Abel Beth-Maakah. They built a siege ramp up to the city, and it stood against the outer fortifications. While they were battering the wall to bring it down, a wise woman called from the city,
> "Listen! Listen! Tell Joab to come here so I can speak to him."
> He went toward her, and she asked, "Are you Joab?"
> "I am," he answered.
> She said, "Listen to what your servant has to say."
> "I'm listening," he said.
> She continued, "Long ago they used to say, 'Get your answer at Abel,' and that settled it. We are the peaceful and faithful in Israel. You are trying to destroy a city that is a mother in Israel. Why do you want to swallow up the Lord's inheritance?"
> "Far be it from me!" Joab replied, "Far be it from me to swallow up or destroy! That is not the case. A man named Sheba

> son of Bikri, from the hill country of Ephraim, has lifted up his hand against the king, against David. Hand over this one man, and I'll withdraw from the city."
>
> The woman said to Joab, "His head will be thrown to you from the wall." Then the woman went to all the people with her wise advice, and they cut off the head of Sheba son of Bikri and threw it to Joab. So, he sounded the trumpet, and his men dispersed from the city, each returning to his home. And Joab went back to the king in Jerusalem." (2 Samuel 20:14–22)

Okay, that is pretty gruesome. Thankfully, we as pastors' wives don't solve problems that way today. Now there might be times . . . no; let's not go there. Nonetheless, saving an entire city is a big deal. It's what I call a major victory. And please understand the magnitude of this situation. Abel Beth-Maakah was not some insignificant small town. It was a fortified city with massive city walls, meaning it was a population center in that region. It was a place of prominence and importance. This "wise woman" changed the game and saved the entire city.

HIS Calling

I have entitled this chapter "HIS Calling" for a reason. When God called our husbands to full-time pastoral ministry, it was HIS (God's) calling on their lives. According to 1 Timothy 3, this is a very special and specific calling. When our men sensed the inward call of the Spirit of God to be a pastor and the outward confirmation from other trusted spiritual leaders, he was essentially being drafted by God to fulfill a specific role for the kingdom of Jesus Christ. Reading through Paul's letters to young the pastor Timothy, we can easily see that HIS calling to pastoral ministry would at times include the inevitability of facing chaos and mayhem—because ministry is a battle.

> But you, man of God, flee from all this, and pursue righteousness, godliness, faith, love, endurance and gentleness. *Fight the good fight of the faith.* Take hold of the eternal life to which you were called when you made your good confession in the presence of many witnesses. (1 Timothy 6:11–12, emphasis added)

Full-time ministry is not comparable to our dodgeball-playing days in gym class with the occasional direct hit to the face. By the way, just that memory still brings tears to my eyes. OUCH! Ministry, as opposed to dodgeball, is not about relatively harmless rubber balls being thrown at one another. The Christian life and ministry life are about facing a ruthless enemy who shoots flaming arrows at everything that is near and dear to our lives.

> For our struggle is not against flesh and blood, but against the rulers, against the authorities, against the powers of this dark world and against the spiritual forces of evil in

> the heavenly realms. Therefore, put on the full armor of God, so that when the day of evil comes, you may be able to stand your ground, and after you have done everything, to stand. Stand firm then, with the belt of truth buckled around your waist, with the breastplate of righteousness in place, and with your feet fitted with the readiness that comes from the gospel of peace. In addition to all this, take up the shield of faith, with which you can extinguish *all the flaming arrows of the evil one*. Take the helmet of salvation and the sword of the Spirit, which is the word of God. (Ephesians 6:12–17, emphasis added)

In dodgeball we might get smashed in the face, only to take five minutes to shake it off, and then on with the rest of our day. In spiritual battles it's real life, real pain, real enemy, real souls, real churches, real friends and real family that are in the line of fire. It's not simply a game; it's a full-on war. HIS calling has to be secure because the full-time-ministry battle is real.

When God sovereignly directed us wives to meet, fall in love with, and join our husbands in HIS calling, it was no accident. HE was also "drafting" us to be a part of this specific and special calling as well. We were uniquely chosen to be a part of God's plan, to come alongside, and to be a vital player on this team. If God called us to marry a pastor, praise God! We're on the team and our pastor needs us!

HIS Calling/Our Calling

One thing that becomes a stark reality soon after entering ministry is this: ministry has the potential to be lonely for both for the husband and the wife. This can be a tremendous hurdle unless the truth of God's Word is embraced, which provides the solution for this problem.

> Then the Lord God said, "It is not good that the man should be alone; I will make him a helper fit for him." (Genesis 2:18)

A pastor and his wife need to be united as a team in order to make it in ministry for the long haul. If either person on the team is not fully engaged, the other will feel the loneliness of doing ministry in isolation, which God's Word says is not good or healthy.

All wives, including pastors' wives, need to understand the importance of our role in our husbands' lives. For him to successfully lead a healthy church, he needs to be a healthy pastor who has a healthy wife. More on that important topic in a later chapter.

Let's reminisce. Do you remember the day you said "I do?" Terry and I met our freshman year in college. It was a God thing that our paths ever crossed in this life. I grew up in Michigan (go Blue), Terry grew up in Iowa. My senior year of high school I had my life all mapped out; that's kind of how I work. I had my Christian college in Ohio selected; I had my career selected, and I had a steady boyfriend. It was a well-thought-out plan that included getting an education, getting married, and becoming a rich businesswoman. The stars were aligned; all that was left was graduating from high school and executing my plan. Then one day my dad had a "good idea" for me to consider. You can always count on a dad to have a "good idea" when you least expect it. Now his good idea wasn't just the mere throwing of a monkey wrench in my carefully crafted plan. It was more like lobbing a lit stick of dynamite into my life that had the potential to blow everything to pieces. His good idea was for me to attend Bible college for a year in Iowa, then circle back and execute my plan. To be honest, I had zero desire to go to a Bible college in the middle of the Iowa corn fields. I had never even been to Iowa. I knew little about it other than it was called the land of corn and swine, and that had no appeal to me at all. As we were processing through his "good idea," I made sure he understood that I would only stay a year and that I was *not* going to marry a pastor. I'm pretty confident I said that more than a few times to make sure he didn't come up with any more "good ideas" before I left for college. He agreed that I did not have to marry a pastor, so I decided to delay my well-thought-out plans for a year and soon loaded up my powder blue station wagon and headed off to Iowa.

My freshman year I met this young, attractive, energetic man named Terry Thompson. We became good friends and nothing more, because I still had a boyfriend back home. As Terry and I got to know each other over that year, it was evident he had little interest in becoming a pastor. He was at college to play basketball and basically have a good time. He was the typical eighteen-year-old adrenaline junky who loved sports, loved life, and had no clue what he wanted to do the next day of his life, let alone the rest of it.

As our freshman year went along, several things began to change. Terry began having feelings for me, and he didn't seem to understand the whole, "boyfriend back at home" thing. By the end of the year, as Terry pursued, God began to change my heart, and eventually I broke up with my boyfriend and began dating Terry. That decision derailed one of the pillars of my previously well-thought-out plan. Then I decided to continue my education in the land of corn and swine past my freshman year. I also decided to change my major from business to elementary education and become a teacher. When our sophomore year rolled around it was evident that Terry and I wanted to spend the rest of our lives together. Then, Terry did the unthinkable. He decided God was calling him to be . . . yes, you guessed it, a pastor! BOOM! The long fuse that my dad lit on that stick of dynamite several years prior exploded. My previously well- thought-out plan was blown to pieces. How could this be happening to me? Then I realized this amazing truth from God's Word:

> The heart of man plans his way, but the Lord establishes his steps. (Proverbs 16:9)

It wasn't my dad that blew up my plans, it was my God redirecting and establishing my steps.

Now, please let me add this about my dad so you don't get the wrong idea. He was a wonderful man! He was a big teddy bear. He loved his four boys but also had a special place in his heart for his little girl. He loved Jesus. He loved his wife, my mom. He loved life. He loved to sing. He was generous. He was the kind of man who never met a stranger. He is in heaven today, and I can't wait to see him again. I miss him. When he was still alive, he loved to reminisce and share the part of the story where his eighteen-year-old daughter emphatically told him "I am *not* going to marry a pastor." And trust me, he shared it with anyone who would listen. We laughed about that memory many times over the years. I will forever be thankful for his godly wisdom that sent me to Iowa and the land of corn and swine.

On June 1, 1985, Terry and I stood before God, family, and friends on our wedding day. During that ceremony I looked deep into Terry's eyes and said these vows from the depth of my heart:

> I, Kelly, take you, Terry, to be my wedded husband; to have and to hold from this day forward, in joy and in sorrow, in sickness and in health, to love and to cherish for the rest of my life. I love you and give myself to you according to God's holy ordinance.

That day and the events leading up to that day changed the course of my life. June 1, 1985 was the day that Terry's calling also became my calling. We became a team. In joy and in sorrow, in sickness and in health, to love and to cherish for the rest of my life. We would from that day on stand side by side, never alone, regardless of how intense the dodgeball games of life and ministry would get.

The Woman of the Word

As I mentioned earlier, it is curious to me that God, in his Word, does not address the role or responsibility of a pastor's wife. Now, I am certainly not questioning God's authoritative Word in any way. I would never intentionally venture down the pathway of doubting God's inspired and inerrant Word. So, in light of this lack of instruction, we need to handle this topic with extreme care so that we do not speak where God's Word does not speak. Therefore, this book will draw our attention to the wife of a leader instead of the wife of a pastor. As we will discover, there are many parallels between the two.

Our focus will be on the wife of a leader as written about in Proverbs 31. Here is what God's Word says about the husband of this wife.

> Her husband is respected at the city gate, where he takes his seat among the elders of the land. (Proverbs 31:23)

A study of the biblical culture reveals that the men who sat at the city gate were the leaders not only of that city but of the entire region. It was a position of prominence and authority. These were men that others looked up to for wisdom and guidance. They were the decision makers. To put it in the setting and vernacular of the day, they were the shepherds of the city.

The Real-life Ministry World

When we married a pastor, we married a shepherd and a leader.

> To the elders among you, I appeal as a fellow elder and a witness of Christ's sufferings who also will share in the glory to be revealed: Be shepherds of God's flock that is under your care, watching over them—not because you must, but because you are willing, as God wants you to be; not pursuing dishonest gain, but eager to serve; not lording it over those entrusted to you, but being examples to the flock. And when the Chief Shepherd appears, you will receive the crown of glory that will never fade away. (1 Peter 5:1–4)

When we married a leader, we married the guy who, when the whistle blows to begin the dodgeball game, fearlessly rushes the center court to grab the nearest ball or two to give his team the advantage. He is a risk taker. He is the enemy's biggest target. He engages the battle while walking the fine line between faith and foolishness. He is a leader; it's what leaders do. When we said, "I do," we joined his team, we sat down and buckled up to ride with him. We promised to be his faithful helper. We might not always like the action of the front lines of the battle, but when it's where God puts our man, we stay with him. It's not just his calling, it's HIS calling for both of us.

The Questions to Wrestle

1. Briefly share your story of how you and your husband met and how God directed you into ministry.
2. Has God ever "redirected your steps" as you have traveled through ministry? What did it look like? How did you handle it?
3. What are your thoughts about your husband's calling also being your calling? Do you agree or disagree and why?
4. The stories of Jael and the "wise woman" demonstrate that God uses women in impactful ways to accomplish His plan. Who are some women in the Bible you admire and why?
5. Share a time it was hard for you to buckle up and faithfully ride with your husband.

CHAPTER 2

MY ASSIGNMENT

The Dodgeball Warriors: "Chaos"

Okay, I got it! I'm on the team. Now what? What is my role? What is my assignment? In dodgeball much of the chaos and mayhem happens because no one is in charge. There is no coach or even a team captain. There is no time given for the team to organize, to strategize, or to have any kind of a game plan at all. There is no allowance to even call a time out if your team is getting pounded by the enemy. When the whistle blows, it's every person for himself. The chaos is immediate and hits like an unexpected tidal wave. In most players it creates an instant response of panic. An immediate adrenalin rush hits and bedlam quickly ensues as people are running everywhere, including teammates running into one another. Others are yelling and screaming at the top of their lungs as balls begin to fly. Some hide behind teammates in an attempt to find a safe haven. Others bunch together thinking a herd mentality will bring safety. From all the various responses, it's safe to say that clear, calm, levelheaded thinking went up in flames at the sound of the whistle.

Looking back at similar life moments, whether it's dodgeball day in gym class or real-life situations, when the chaos hits, it's hard to think clearly and rationally. It's just how our human brains are wired. In times of bedlam, basic survival instincts automatically begin kicking in. We say to ourselves, "Do what you think is right. Do what you think is best for you. Just stay alive as long as you can." Its complete self-preservation.

It reminds me of how the nation of Israel responded in the dark days of the Judges. Reading the biblical text would indicate an endless cycle of chaos and mayhem. What would have possibly caused this to be the norm? God's Word tells us that as the nation of Israel wandered away from God, He left them to figure things out on their own. The end result of this was almost always tragic. Here is how the book of Judges ends.

> In those days Israel had no king; everyone did as they saw fit. (Judges 21:25)

We all understand the ramifications of trying to do things that are just "best for me." In Judges it literally created hundreds of years of chaos. Hundreds of years of a massive dodgeball game. Everyone doing what was right in their own eyes for their self-preservation.

Today, it reminds me of stores opening their doors on black Friday. It's a shopping frenzy the day after Thanksgiving. Personally, my girls, Katie and Holly, and I have joined the crazies and love it. We go every chance we get. There is this weird kind of fun insanity to the whole thing. However, it is dangerous to throw caution to the wind. Things can quickly turn into pandemonium.

We have all seen the results of human selfishness in these moments as people fend for themselves and do what seems best for them, regardless of the pain it might cause others! What do marketing people think will happen when hundreds of shoppers vie for the five televisions on sale for $99? Yes, people actually get injured every year.

We see the same thing in a good old dodgeball game. Without someone being in charge, people can get out of control very quickly. It doesn't take long when observing these kinds of scenarios to realize the importance of order and structure. That is why it's important for us to bring clarity to our assignment.

The Real-life Ministry World

Thankfully, in God's plans there is always order and structure. God is not a God of chaos and confusion. From the very beginning of creation until the final events in Revelation, his plan is meticulously ordered.

> For God is not a God of disorder but of peace. (1 Corinthians 14:33a)

I find great comfort in the fact that our God establishes needed leadership structure for key areas of life like government, households, and his church.

Knowing our pastor/husband is called to lead God's church brings great clarity to the church and those serving under his care. It's part of God's plan to keep his church from turning into a chaotic dodgeball game. Thank God for our pastors.

But the million-dollar question for us wives is this: What is my role and my assignment? I know I'm on the team and in the game, but where do I go from there? I need to get rid of this stinking blindfold!

When a challenging topic is brought up, have you ever heard someone say, "You didn't really go there?" It's the idea that you opened the proverbial can of worms, that you went where angels fear to tread. Well, yes, we are going there, so hang on.

One of our key assignments as a pastor's wife is to be a leader. Yes, a leader. Pastors' wives occasionally resist this idea. Sometimes they push back by saying their husband was called to be the leader, not them. This is true in many ways and on many levels; however, any time a person has a position where people look up to them, that is a position of leadership. Terry, for example, loves to be large and in charge. He is not afraid of the spotlight. In fact, it energizes him. I would prefer never to be in the spotlight at all. I'm great with being a behind-the-scenes pastor's wife. Even writing this book makes me nauseous because I understand it has the potential to put me in a spotlight. Friends, here is our reality, like it or not: we are married to leaders; therefore, we will always be viewed as a leader as well. Certainly, our biblical roles and responsibilities are different than that of our husbands, but our standing before others will always be one of leadership. Recognizing we are in a leadership role helps clarify our assignment.

My husband, Terry, besides being a pastor, has also been a certified leadership coach for many years. He has often repeated this definition of leadership:

> Leadership is a behavior that influences others and drives an outcome. (Lyle Wells, President, Integrus Leadership)

As pastors' wives, and as a person that others look up to, our behaviors do influence others and they do assist in driving many outcomes. Some may be positive and others negative. Because of our assignment as pastors' wives, we must own our behaviors, our influence, and the corresponding outcomes. Our behaviors communicate loudly. If a young man is known by his behaviors, so is a pastor's wife.

> Even a young man is known by his actions—by whether his behavior is pure and upright. (Proverbs 20:11 CSB)

The Woman of the Word

The Proverbs 31 woman was a leader. She made decisions. She engaged with the team. She did not sit back un-noticed. She was active, responsible, and productive. Look at how Proverbs describes what she does,

> Proverbs 31:13a: She selects wool and flax
> Proverbs 31:15a: She gets up while it is still night
> Proverbs 31: 15b: She provides food for her family
> Proverbs 31:16a: She considers a field and buys it
> Proverbs 31:17a: She sets about her work vigorously
> Proverbs 31:18a: She sees that her trading is profitable
> Proverbs 31:20a: She opens her arms to the poor
> Proverbs 31:21a: She has no fear for her household
> Proverbs 31:22a: She makes coverings for her bed
> Proverbs 31:24a: She makes linen garments and sells them
> Proverbs 31:25a: She is clothed with strength and dignity
> Proverbs 31:26a: She speaks with wisdom
> Proverbs 31:27a: She watches over the affairs of her household

I don't know about you, but I am tired just reading all that she did! Very impressive.

Was she a leader? Did she take initiative? Did her leadership behaviors influence others and drive outcomes? Yes, it is why she was praised.

> Her children arise and call her blessed; her husband also, and he praises her.
>
> . . .
>
> Honor her for all that her hands have done, and let her works bring her praise at the city gate. (Proverbs 31:28, 31)

Leadership is a behavior. God's Word overflows with examples of behaviors, sinful and righteous, that have influenced others and driven their respective outcomes. How about a quick Bible study and some examples to drive home the point? As we look at the following passages, look for the behavior, the influence, and the outcome. All of these passages deal with women in the Bible.

Eve's sinful behavior in the garden of Eden had an immediate influence and a domino effect of tragic outcomes. Even today we deal with the outcomes of her decisions.

> When the woman saw that the fruit of the tree was good for food and pleasing to the eye, and also desirable for gaining wisdom, she took some and ate it. She also gave some to her husband, who was with her, and he ate it. (Genesis 3:6)

> Therefore, just as sin entered the world through one man, and death through sin, and in this way death came to all people, because all sinned. (Romans 5:12)

The sinful behavior of Potiphar's wife influenced her husband and it drove the outcome of landing an innocent man, Joseph, in jail for many years.

> She kept his cloak beside her until his master came home. Then she told him this story: "That Hebrew slave you brought us came to me to make sport of me. But as soon as I screamed for help, he left his cloak beside me and ran

> out of the house." When his master heard the story his wife told him, saying, "This is how your slave treated me," he burned with anger. Joseph's master took him and put him in prison, the place where the king's prisoners were confined. (Genesis 39:16–20a)

Esther's righteous behaviors, at personal risk to her life, influenced a king and drove the outcome of saving the Jewish nation from certain destruction. The background to the story is this: wicked Haman manipulated the King into signing a decree that would wipe out the Jewish people. God had strategically placed Esther as the queen, "for such a time as this."

However, even with the title of queen, she did not have open access to the king at any time. When she approached him to plead for her people, she was putting her life in grave danger. If he did not extend his golden scepter and invite her in, her life may have been taken.

> On the third day Esther put on her royal robes and stood in the inner court of the palace, in front of the king's hall. The king was sitting on his royal throne in the hall, facing the entrance. When he saw Queen Esther standing in the court, he was pleased with her and held out to her the gold scepter that was in his hand. So, Esther approached and touched the tip of the scepter. Then the king asked, "What is it, Queen Esther? What is your request? Even up to half the kingdom, it will be given you." (Esther 5:1–3)

Naomi's righteous behaviors influenced Ruth and

drove the outcome of being rescued by a kinsman redeemer. Who knew uncovering someone's feet could be life changing?

> One day Ruth's mother-in-law Naomi said to her, "My daughter, I must find a home for you, where you will be well provided for. Now Boaz, with whose women you have worked, is a relative of ours. Tonight he will be winnowing barley on the threshing floor. Wash, put on perfume, and get dressed in your best clothes. Then go down to the threshing floor, but don't let him know you are there until he has finished eating and drinking. When he lies down, note the place where he is lying. Then go and uncover his feet and lie down. He will tell you what to do." (Ruth 3:1–4)

Mary's righteous behaviors in the midst of an unexpected pregnancy influenced a nation and drove an outcome of being the mother of the Lord Jesus Christ.

> The angel answered, "The Holy Spirit will come on you, and the power of the Most High will overshadow you. So the holy one to be born will be called the Son of God. Even Elizabeth your relative is going to have a child in her old age, and she who was said to be unable to conceive is in her sixth month. For no word from God will ever fail."
>
> "I am the Lord's servant," Mary answered. "May your word to me be fulfilled." Then the angel left her. (Luke 1:35–38)

Solomon had many wives; their sinful behaviors influenced the king to worship and sacrifice to the foreign gods of foreign nations. This drove the outcome of God's punishment of Solomon's family line and eventually a divided kingdom.

> As Solomon grew old, his wives turned his heart after other gods, and his heart was not fully devoted to the Lord his God, as the heart of David his father had been. He followed Ashtoreth the goddess of the Sidonians, and Molek the detestable god of the Ammonites. So Solomon did evil in the eyes of the Lord; he did not follow the Lord completely, as David his father had done. (1 Kings 11:4–6)

Abigail's righteous behaviors influenced David and drove the outcome of saving her husband, Nabal, from certain death at the hand of David.

> When Abigail saw David, she quickly got off her donkey and bowed down before David with her face to the ground. She fell at his feet and said: "Pardon your servant, my lord, and let me speak to you; hear what your servant has to say. Please pay no attention, my lord, to that wicked man Nabal. He is just like his name—his name means Fool, and folly goes with him. And as for me, your servant, I did not see the men my lord sent. And now, my lord, as surely as the Lord your God lives and as you live, since the Lord has kept you from bloodshed and from avenging yourself with your own hands, may your enemies and all who are intent on harming my lord be like Nabal." (1 Samuel 25:23–26)

Ananias and Sapphira's sinful behaviors influenced each other and drove the outcome of the loss of their lives.

> Now a man named Ananias, together with his wife Sapphira, also sold a piece of property. With his wife's full knowledge, he kept back part of the money for himself, but brought the rest and put it at the apostles' feet. "Ananias," Peter asked, "why has Satan filled your heart to lie to the Holy Spirit and keep back part of the proceeds of the land? Wasn't it yours while you possessed it? And after it was sold, wasn't it at your disposal? Why is it that you planned this thing in your heart? You have not lied to people but to God." When he heard these words, Ananias dropped dead, and a great fear came on all who heard.
>
> The young men got up, wrapped his body, carried him out, and buried him. About three hours later, his wife came in, not knowing what had happened. "Tell me," Peter asked her, "did you sell the land for this price?" "Yes," she said, "for that price." Then Peter said to her, "Why did you agree to test the Spirit of the Lord? Look, the feet of those who have buried your husband are at the door, and they will carry you out." Instantly she dropped dead at his feet. When the young men came in, they found her dead, carried her out, and buried her beside her husband. (Acts 5:1–10)

Athaliah's was the mother of King Ahaziah. Her behaviors were so wicked that they negatively influenced the kingdom and drove the outcome of the people actually celebrating her death.

> When Athaliah the mother of Ahaziah saw that her son was dead, she proceeded to destroy the whole royal family of the house of Judah. (2 Chronicles 22:10)

> All the people of the land rejoiced, and the city was calm, because Athaliah had been slain with the sword at the palace. (2 Kings 11:20)

An unnamed woman had the insight to realize that Elisha was a man of God. She then persuaded her husband into showing Elisha kindness, even providing a room for him in their home. This behavior influenced the prophet and eventually drove the outcome of saving her dead son's life.

> One day Elisha went to Shunem. And a well-to-do woman was there, who urged him to stay for a meal. So whenever he came by, he stopped there to eat. She said to her husband, "I know that this man who often comes our way is a holy man of God. Let's make a small room on the roof and put in it a bed and a table, a chair and a lamp for him. Then he can stay there whenever he comes to us." (2 Kings 4:8–10)
>
> . . .
>
> When Elisha reached the house, there was the boy lying dead on his couch. He went in, shut the door on the two of them and prayed to the Lord. Then he got on the bed and lay on the boy, mouth to mouth, eyes to eyes, hands to hands. As he stretched himself out on him, the boy's body grew warm. Elisha turned away and walked back and forth in the room and then got on the bed and stretched

> out on him once more. The boy sneezed seven times and opened his eyes. Elisha summoned Gehazi and said, "Call the Shunammite. And he did. When she came, he said, "Take your son." She came in, fell at his feet and bowed to the ground. Then she took her son and went out. (2 Kings 4:8-10, 32-37)

At times you save the best for last, well this might be saving the worst for last. How about Queen Jezebel? Her wicked behaviors influenced her husband, King Ahab, which led to the outcome of the nation of Israel living in deep sin before the Lord. This sinful influence lasted for generations with God's people.

> There was never anyone like Ahab, who sold himself to do evil in the eyes of the Lord, urged on by Jezebel his wife. He behaved in the vilest manner by going after idols, like the Amorites the Lord drove out before Israel. (1 Kings 21:25-26)

Leadership is a behavior that influences others and drives an outcome. Don't you love that definition? It's so true, and it's easily seen and applied. Now, let's start at the beginning of that definition. When we address the topic of behaviors, we need to look at the deeper issues of the heart. God's Word instructs us that behaviors flow from the heart. When there are behavioral issues, there are also heart issues.

> But the things that come out of a person's mouth come from the heart, and these defile them. For out of the heart

> come evil thoughts—murder, adultery, sexual immorality, theft, false testimony, slander. (Matthew 15:18–19)

The outward behaviors of our lives stem from one source. The heart. Therefore, keeping our hearts in line with God and his Word is paramount in our lives. As Proverbs 4:23 says, "Above all else, guard your heart, for everything you do flows from it."

Now, back to the topic of leadership. Let's do a quick litmus test and see if there is adequate evidence to support the notion that we are in fact leaders. Here is our question, "Are my behaviors and attitudes influencing others and driving outcomes?" The answer is an absolute, "Yes!" If we sense that some of our behaviors are not pleasing to Christ, then it's time to go back and check the heart that Psalm 139:23–24 recommends: "Search me, God, and know my heart; test me and know my anxious thoughts. See if there is any offensive way in me, and lead me in the way everlasting." If you're anything like me, with a sinful and selfish heart that is prone to wander, then doing this heart check thing can be a bit painful, but it is absolutely necessary. How's your heart?

I pray this chapter helped you remove the blindfold, or at least loosened it up enough so you could peek out and get a glimpse of daylight. Let's be honest; when it came to blindfold games as kids, we all know we cheated and peeked a time or two. This is what we discovered: just a small amount of vision was extremely helpful in bringing clarity to the unknown.

Understanding that our assignment involves being viewed as a leader brings some needed clarity to our position. Like the Proverbs 31 woman, we should not fear the role God has called us to fulfill. We should follow her example. We should engage with the team. We should not expect to be completely unnoticed. We should be active, responsible, and productive. Please do not be afraid of the term "leader." It does not infer you are attempting to overstep your God-given boundaries or authorities. It simply means that others are watching. It means you are an influencer. It means you may impact outcomes more than others simply because of your position as a pastor's wife.

The Questions to Wrestle

1. What are your thoughts about being labeled as a leader? Does that excite you or make you nervous? Why?
2. Definition: "Leadership is a behavior that influences others and drives an outcome."
   Share some examples of where you have seen this demonstrated in your life. Share one good and one not so good example.
3. Definition: "Leadership is a behavior that influences others and drives an outcome."
   Discuss how you have seen the good and bad of this played out in the leadership of our current society and culture.
4. Which one of the "good" examples of the women we listed in the chapter most inspires you and why?
5. What are some practical ways you can guard your heart so that your behaviors are pleasing to Christ?

CHAPTER 3

HIS GOOD

The Dodgeball Warriors: "The Good Team Player"

There are lots of ways to be a good team player, and likewise, there are many ways to be a bad team player. Good team players are easy to identify. They cheer others on regardless if they are on the floor or sitting on the bench, having already been eliminated. They have fun. They have their other teammates' backs. Their attitude is positive. They play hard. When they are on your team its always more enjoyable. Win or lose, put me on that team any day. A bad team player is exactly the opposite. They hog the ball. They are selfish. Their attitude stinks. They are easily discouraged. They don't think about the welfare of others. It's all about them. When they are on your team it's like a dark cloud is hovering over your head and your team. Not an enjoyable experience. No thanks.

So, let's talk about how important it is that we are good team players as we partner with our husbands in ministry. Let's be the ray of sunshine that infuses the team with energy and not the dark cloud that sucks the life out of people.

The Woman of the Word

I continue to cherish the truths listed in Proverbs 31. The wife in the text is the wife of a leader. We know by this verse that she is the ray of sunshine, and I love it!

> She brings him good, not harm, all the days of her life. (Proverbs 31:12)

Wow! What a great team player! Her attitude is to simply bring good and not harm, to the one she loves most in her life. Trust me, if our husbands knew that was our goal, and we actually accomplished that goal, they would be inspired and encouraged daily. Not to mention we might get a few more dates, flowers, cards, and of course the life-essential and life-giving chocolate. BAM! Big wins for the entire team!

And let's not overlook this truth: it is pleasing to Christ when we live a life of goodness. It's part of living a life exemplified by the fruit of the Spirit:

> But the fruit of the Spirit is love, joy, peace, forbearance, kindness, goodness, faithfulness, gentleness and self-control. (Galatians 5:22–23a)

I think we would all agree that as we strive to fulfill this mission, we will experience great personal joy as well as satisfaction knowing we are bringing good fruit to the team. Here is the reason we can bring good fruit. It is because Proverbs reminds us that we are a good addition to our husband's team:

> He who finds a wife finds what is good and receives favor from the Lord. (Proverbs 18:22)

So, let's flesh this out. How do we bring our husbands good and not harm as we partner with them in ministry? We will explore several more of these possibilities in the following chapters, but let's explore this area first.

Are we doing him good by being *all in*? Are we fully engaged with our husbands in HIS calling to pastoral ministry? The answer to those all-important questions will play a significant role in the long-term health of the church. Our attitude toward his calling and our assignment will influence him and drive an outcome. Our experience over the years would indicate that pastors without wives who are all in will eventually struggle in their calling.

The Real-Life Ministry World

As Terry and I have served in full-time pastoral ministry since 1985, we have worked alongside many other pastors and wives who have served on our teams. Most of them have been amazing and continue to be dear friends with us yet today. They are part of our family. We have been abundantly blessed over the years. They have modeled Christ-like teamwork in the midst of ministry calm and chaos. Through all of these years there have also been a scarce few who have struggled because their wives were not all in. When this is the case, it creates a weight for the husband/pastor that will eventually take its toll. His ministry health will diminish as his wife's attitudes and behaviors diminish. The result is always the same; the negative behaviors have a profound influence and drive a sad ending.

Over the years, as along with observing our pastoral team members, I have also played a role in the interview and hiring process of new pastors to fill open spots on our teams. My assignment in this was not to interview the potential pastor but to take a few close friends and spend some time with the pastor's wife. It's amazing what you can learn while casually sipping a delicious cup of caramel macchiato at a coffee shop with friends. One of the goals of these meetings was to gauge the wife's interest in full-time ministry. It was perplexing at times to hear a wife talk as if her husband was called to ministry but that his calling was somehow disconnected from her goals, dreams, and desires. It's a subtle attitude of, "He does his thing and I do mine." Needless to say, we did not hire a single one of those prospects. An absentee member of the team is not an asset but rather a liability.

Let's look at some practical areas where the rubber meets the road. Here are some ways I believe pastors' wives can bring their husbands good and not harm as they fulfill their assignment.

Love God

There are no words to adequately convey the importance of keeping our relationship with God on track. Will there be challenging days, weeks, months, or seasons? Will there be days we are tired and at our wits' end? Will there be days of sickness? Days of discouragement? Days of heartache? Days of failure? Days of wanting to wave the white flag of surrender? Days of wanting to throw in the towel? Yes! I have been there many times over the decades that we have been in ministry. And, I am guessing, so have you. Where do we turn? What do we do? How do we climb out of those deep and dark holes? Since we can all be honest enough to admit to those days, let's be encouraged by this thought. King David knew those days as well. I guess if one of God's most prominent, chosen kings can be vulnerable enough to admit to the struggle, then so can we. In his dark days, David always found strength to get back in the game from one particular place. His number-one plan was to retreat and spend time with his God and the truth of God's Word.

> I waited patiently for the Lord; he turned to me and heard my cry. He lifted me out of the slimy pit, out of the mud and mire; he set my feet on a rock and gave me a firm place to stand. He put a new song in my mouth, a hymn of praise to our God. Many will see and fear the Lord and put their trust in him. (Psalm 40:1–3)

Oh, there is that waiting patiently thing. Yeah, I'm not so good at that either. But I do like the idea that, when the waiting is over, there is victory to be enjoyed. Crawling out of the slimy pit and standing on a solid rock sure sounds like a win to me. Not to mention feeling like singing again and being a testimony to others. Win! Win! Win!

Years ago, Terry and I entered an event called the Warrior Dash, a three-mile run with multiple obstacles and challenges to face before crossing the finish line. It was a fun event, with hundreds of people participating. It was also enjoyable because the goal was not to be the first to cross the finish line but simply to complete the race successfully. That was the win. After we ran, climbed walls, swung on ropes, completed monkey bars, high stepped through tires, swam through a cow-pasture pond, and jumped over fire, we neared the end of the course. As we came around the last turn, there before us was the final obstacle. A huge mud pit with a meshed wire stretched about twelve inches over the entire length of the pit. It forced you into the mud. There were no other options. The finish line was only accessible through the mud. As we slowly lowered ourselves into the muck and mire, the only part of our bodies that were not immersed in the slime was our heads. It was nasty! With the trench able to accommodate about four people wide, there was mud being slung in every direction. People were in pure survival mode so as to not fall prey to the last obstacle. It was now the final push, finish or die, and who wants to have their obituary read, "death by mud"? Since there was no way to cross the finish line without going through the dreaded mud pit, we sloshed on! Once we got to the end and crawled our way out of the other side, there was only one thing left: to cross the finish line. Then the event organizers proudly hung the coveted Warrior Dash medal around our necks and the celebration began. We high-fived our friends, took pictures, and shared our valiant exploits with all who would listen. It was a memorable Saturday morning. Then we headed for home and enjoyed a long, hot shower! Oh, it never felt so good!

One of the lessons I learned from the Warrior Dash was this: sometimes there is no way around the mud pits of life and ministry. You will get sucked in; you have no choice. It will be nasty, it is disgusting, and you will get dirty. But just like there is a beginning to the mud pit, there is also an end. Once you finally crawl out of the mire, there is reason to rejoice, celebrate, and testify to others. That is exactly what King David experienced when he finally climbed out of the mud and mire and found the solid rock and a new song. God is the solid Rock to whom David was referring in

Psalm 40. He mentions that name for God over fifty times in the book of Psalms. He also named God as his Rock after being pursued by King Saul, who was looking to take his life.

> David sang to the Lord the words of this song when the Lord delivered him from the hand of all his enemies and from the hand of Saul. He said: "The Lord is my rock, my fortress and my deliverer; my God is my rock, in whom I take refuge, my shield and the horn of my salvation. He is my stronghold, my refuge and my savior— from violent people you save me. I called to the Lord, who is worthy of praise, and have been saved from my enemies." (2 Samuel 22:1–4)

Doing our husbands good and not harm is accomplished when we take as short a stay as possible in the slimy pit. It's not a matter of if we are going to face the mud, because eventually we all will. It's a matter of how long we are going to stay there. Loving God means rediscovering our joyful heart and voice after getting stuck in the mire. Terry's grandpa was an old gospel preacher who used to call this psalm, "Out of the mire and into the choir." I like that! Let's keep doing him good and singing as we go.

Love Him

Attention and affection are two more ways we can do our husbands good and not harm. Our men are men.

If we have been married, even for a short time, we know they are suckers for our love and attention. I remember being at a couple's retreat where our dear friends Randy and Cindy Patten were the keynote speakers. During the session on wives paying attention to their husbands, the sex talk, if you will, they displayed Ephesians 5:33b from the Amplified Bible and it reads like this:

> and let the wife see that she respects and reverences her husband that she notices him, regards him, honors him, prefers him, venerates, and esteems him; and that she defers to him, praises him, and loves and admires him exceedingly. (Ephesians 5:33b AMPC)

The comment from Cindy following the reading of that verse is what I will never forget. "Ladies, your husband will charge Hell with a water pistol for a wife that loves him like that!" That is how much attention and affection mean to our husbands. If we do not love him physically, we will never convince him that we are truly on his team.

> Solomon reminds us of this as well,
> Drink water from your own cistern, running water from your own well.
> Should your springs overflow in the streets, your streams of water in the public squares? Let them be yours alone, never to be shared with strangers. May your fountain be blessed, and may you rejoice in the wife of your youth. A loving doe,

> a graceful deer—may her breasts satisfy you always, may you ever be intoxicated with her love. (Proverbs 5:15–19)

These verses usually get applied to men in regard to staying faithful to their wives, and rightfully so; however, look at the last phrase. It says, "May you ever be intoxicated with her love." Maybe our question to ask is this, how intoxicating is my love to my husband? Personally, some days I feel like I'm 100-proof and other days about as zippy as a drink of water. And once again a little transparency—I know about the 100-proof thing from my B.C. days (before Christ), so let's not judge or throw stones, just saying. But seriously, let's make sure we are bringing at least a little punch to our love for our man. It is important, and here is why. As a leader he will also get attention from others because he is in the spotlight. It is what it is. However, the attention he desires the most is from you. There is only one person he can love intimately and only one person who can love him intimately, without him falling into sin, and that is his wife. Doing him good and not harm can be accomplished by making sure our love for him is consistent and compelling.

Engage Him

Terry is an adventurer. Me, not so much. He is a thrill seeker and enjoys pushing the limits. He has hiked the Grand Canyon, jumped out of a perfectly good plane on three separate occasions, traveled to remote parts of the Amazon rain forest on a missions trip, crawled through caves, explored off-limit places in Israel, and spent many years leading groups to Canada on wilderness trips. Yes, he loves a new adventure and for some reason always thinks the signs like "do not enter," "danger," and "stay out" mean the place is hiding something really cool that he just needs to see. That is my guy. He has always enjoyed the road less traveled and probably always will. Me? That's not how I am wired. My thinking is why would a person jump out of perfectly good airplane? Why would a person sit in a small tree stand for hours in subzero temperatures while waiting for a deer to walk by? Why would a person take bread with him while snorkeling, only to sprinkle it in the water and thus intentionally cause a fish feeding frenzy all around him? Why? That is not how I am wired; it's just not me. But I have learned this over the years. I can do him good and not harm in two ways.

First, I can let him have his adventures without being the nagging wife.

> An endless dripping on a rainy day and a nagging wife are alike. (Proverbs 27:15a)

Now I will admit that I have given him "the look" a few times when I think he might be pushing a little too close to the edge. But most of the time, I smile and let him enjoy his adventures. You see, he is a storyteller at heart, and he loves to share his exploits. And, yes; the tales get bigger as the years go by. But don't tell him I said that.

Second, I have discovered that engaging him how God wired him has brought a lot of excitement to my life as well. Sometimes I employ the old adage, "If you can't beat them join them." So, occasionally I will venture out of my safe little box and join in on some of his craziness. Like participating with him in the Warrior Dash. On another occasion he talked me into snorkeling with him in the crystal-clear waters surrounding a volcanic island. The water was unusually warm because streams of bubbles cascaded up from the deep blue depths due to the volcanic heat under the surface of the ocean floor. I just kept thinking to myself, "I sure hope the volcano doesn't decide to erupt today!" Thankfully, we lived to tell about it and made a great memory.

Your guy is not my guy. Your guy has his things, his talents, his interests, his guy things. If you will engage with him in whatever those things are, it will help build the team. Any time we help build the team we are doing him good and not harm. Allowing our married lives to drift apart because of differing interests is very dangerous. It's not only a marriage yellow flag; it's a marriage red flag. Engage with him and enjoy the adventure.

Refresh Him

Ministry is about people. People are wonderful and life giving. People are also challenging and life draining. Ministry is fun and exciting. Ministry is also hard and challenging. Sometimes it may seem as if you are on the losing team of the ministry dodgeball game, with a never-expiring score clock. Will the chaos ever end? Will the mayhem ever stop? Thankfully, this does not describe nor encompass the normal daily life in the pastoral world, but it might describe seasons. One significant way to do our husbands good and not harm is to make sure our home is a place of retreat in the midst of the storm. Sometimes he just needs a quick trip into the calm eye of the hurricane before the wind blows again.

God knew Elijah had been in the heat of the battle on Mount Carmel. The wicked Queen Jezebel was seeking to take his life after her false prophets were discredited and executed. As Elijah fled for his life God meets him as he hid in the cleft of a mountain.

> The Lord said, "Go out and stand on the mountain in the presence of the Lord, for the Lord is about to pass by." Then a great and powerful wind tore the mountains apart and shattered the rocks before the Lord, but the Lord was not in the wind. After the wind there was an earthquake, but the Lord was not in the earthquake. After the earthquake came a fire, but the Lord was not in the fire. And after the fire came a gentle whisper. (1 Kings 19:11–12)

How refreshing can a gentle whisper be in the midst of the chaos? Elijah needed it, and so do our husbands at times. Our home is our safe place. It's the calm eye in the center of the hurricane. A place of gentle whispers. In a world of chaos, our homes are an important place.

Here are ten areas where we can make sure our home is a place of refreshment. These are not only a wife's responsibilities; these are a family's responsibility. Teamwork! But many times, the wife will be the one to set the vision for these things to become a reality.

- Clean: Cleanliness is refreshing
- Clutter free: Simple is better
- Family focused: Eating together is encouraging
- Fun: Find many reasons to laugh
- Organized: Everything needs a place
- Quiet: Turn off the electronics
- Uninterrupted: Screen calls with voicemail—most things can wait until tomorrow
- Routine: keep the kids' schedules organized
- Fixed: Repairs and remodeling are life giving . . . when they are finished
- Relaxed: Work will be there tomorrow

Are we after the perfect utopia in our homes? Not a chance. Perfection is not the goal because perfection is not sustainable over the long haul. My son-in-law, Brad, who is a football coach, once shared this phrase with us: "Aim for perfection and you will often hit excellence."

Set the goal high for your home environment. It is a great way to bring your husband good and not harm.

Represent Him

How we conduct ourselves in public is another way we can do him good and not harm. The leader's wife in Proverbs 31 represented her husband well:

> Her husband has full confidence in her and lacks nothing of value. (Proverbs 31:11)

He is not worried about her conduct when he is not around. He is not worried that she will step out of line or embarrass him in any way. In fact, he has full confidence that in all she does, she will add tremendous value to the team. That is certainly a badge of honor that will bring him good and not harm.

The Bible is not complimentary of women whose conduct is out of line with Christlikeness.

> Like a gold ring in a pig's snout is a beautiful woman who shows no discretion." (Proverbs 11:22)

Now that's a vivid imagery. Certainly not a compliment.

> Besides, they get into the habit of being idle and going about from house to house. And not only do they become idlers,

> but also busybodies who talk nonsense, saying things they ought not to. (1 Timothy 5:13)

So, let's not be busybodies, okay? Let's address how and when we speak. It is a way to bring our husbands good, or it is a way to bring them much harm. As pastors' wives we have to learn how to smile and not say all the things our brains are sending to our tongues. Oh, that is so not easy! There are many times I just want to say it! It's that sarcastic thing. But I should not. I must not. Solomon reminds us of this truth:

> Sin is not ended by multiplying words, but the prudent hold their tongues. (Proverbs 10:19)

James also reminds us of this truth:

> My dear brothers and sisters, take note of this: Everyone should be quick to listen, slow to speak and slow to become angry, because human anger does not produce the righteousness that God desires. (James 1:19–20)

Terry often lovingly reminds me that "sarcasm is not a spiritual gift." I have yet to find the chapter and verse that supports his claim, so for me the jury is still out. I can't even tell you how many times I have a good one-liner that would perfectly fit the occasion, only to swallow it down and just smile. There is some of that honesty I talked about in my introduction. Yes, there are times it is challenging; but when I remember my assignment, it helps guide me to the proper decision. I not only represent Christ, but I also represent my husband. My assignment is to bring him good and not harm.

Let's also take a moment to address social media. What a double-edged sword. So much potential for good and so much potential for harm. A good friend of ours once gave us this advice. Write about good things; talk about bad things. What wisdom there is in that statement. Never put bad things into writing because when we do, there is always the potential it will resurface and cause damage. Use social media for all the good it can accomplish, but don't allow it to be the avenue for venting or making your statement. Those emotional decisions always tend to eventually bring a bad outcome.

My assignment is to bring him good and not harm. That biblical principle is important, and it does make a difference.

> A wife of noble character is her husband's crown, but a disgraceful wife is like decay in his bones. (Proverbs 12:4)

The Questions to Wrestle

This chapter talked about five ways to do your husband good and not harm. Let's focus on those.

1. Love God. What are some ways your husband can visibly see that your love relationship with God is strong and consistent?
2. Have you ever fallen into the slimy pit? What took you there and how did you get out?
3. Love Him. How's your love life? Not too many details please. How are you intoxicating to your husband?
4. Engage him. What man things does your husband enjoy? How is he wired? In what ways do you engage with him in order to build the team?
5. Refresh him. Kelly listed ten ways to refresh our husbands. List the one you believe you do the best and the one you need to work on the most. What else would you add to this list?
6. Represent him. What are some practical ways we can represent Christ and our husbands by not saying what we really want to say? How do you find victory in this area?

CHAPTER 4

THEIR EXPECTATIONS

The Dodgeball Warriors - "That Guy"

So many times in life there is "that guy." I think we know what I mean when I use that phrase. It's the person you pray you never become. They are the know-it-all, tell everyone what to do, I'm always right, don't second guess me, fall in line, and do-what-I-tell-you-to- do, kind of a person. It's the guy Proverbs refers to as the mocker. Even Solomon says, that you don't want to be "that guy"!

> Whoever corrects a mocker invites insults; whoever rebukes the wicked incurs abuse. Do not rebuke mockers or they will hate you. (Proverbs 9:7–8a)

> Mockers resent correction, so they avoid the wise. (Proverbs 15:12)

> The proud and arrogant person—"Mocker" is his name—behaves with insolent fury. (Proverbs 21:24)

I am so fearful of even slightly resembling that person that sometimes I want to wear a t-shirt that says,

"Please let me know if I am being 'that guy.'" Almost every group has "that guy," yes, even middle school gym class. Many times it's the good looking, athletic, macho boy who somehow got the idea that he was God's gift to mankind, or at least to his middle school. On dodgeball day it usually goes something like this: When teams are divided, he begins laying out the game plan and telling everyone what to do. If someone challenges his self-given authority, he either responds in anger or shrugs the challenger off and moves on. Then, in the heat of the game, if his directives are not followed and something goes wrong, he is all too eager to blame one of the other team members. Since dodgeball has very few rules, there really isn't a right or wrong way to play the game. The only thing that is perceived as wrong is if a person is not following through on the self-appointed leader's expectations. When his plan fails and he takes it out on others, that often leads to intense arguments and infighting among the team.

Their Expectations

Being a pastor's wife can also be challenging when it comes to expectations. Many people within the congregation have their expectations of what a job description for the pastor's wife should look like. In the mid-1980s when Terry and I were beginning ministry, there were many varying expectations of how and where a pastor's wife should serve within the church, depending on the church and the people. The word that comes to my mind is nebulous, "unclear, vague, or ill-defined."

Nonetheless, the expectations were real. It was almost expected that she played the piano for corporate worship, headed up children's ministries, lead women's Bible studies, was the church secretary, and ran the ever-important church kitchen. Now, maybe that is a bit of an exaggeration, but then again, maybe it's not?

Let's see if we can bring some clarity to the unclear, vague, and ill-defined specifics of a job description for a pastor's wife. What does God's Word say? To simplify the matter, let's list the top five most important responsibilities.

1.
2.
3.
4.
5.

And there you have it! Now, you might be thinking we forgot to fill in the blanks. In actuality we did list everything God's Word has to say about the responsibilities of a pastor's wife. There is no list. There are no specific details. The job description is blank. Of course, we must acknowledge that we have the same responsibilities as all other Christ followers. We are to love God and love others, serve God and serve others. Other than that, there is much liberty and grace for how a pastor's wife serves within the context of her husband's ministry calling.

Terry has always been very clear about this area to our church family when a pastor and his wife have joined our ministry team. During their installment service, he makes a point to address the specific job description of the pastor. Then he addresses the pastor's wife. He makes certain the church understands that her primary role is to love her husband and family and then to serve as Christ would expect any of our church members to serve and participate. Above that, there are no biblical expectations given.

Freedom in Serving

I would like to encourage all of us pastors' wives to live in the freedom of God's grace in this area. He has created each one of us differently when it comes to our giftedness and passions. Please do not try to live up to the expectations of others. No one can handle the weight of that pressure. Please live up to the expectations of your loving heavenly Father. It is he who gifted you and created you to do good works in his name. Live up to his expectations. As Paul reminds us in Ephesians,

> For we are God's handiwork, created in Christ Jesus to do good works, which God prepared in advance for us to do. (Ephesians 2:10)

Over the years I have learned to live in that grace-filled freedom and pursue the passions Christ has laid on my heart. It hasn't always been easy because I like people to like me. It's a continual temptation to wonder what they are thinking. Am I living up to their expectations? What if I disappoint them? Am I representing what a pastor's wife should be? The pressure can be immense, but living under God's freeing grace reminds me that ultimately, someday, I must stand before my God—and not man—and give an account for how I used my passions and gifts for his church and his glory.

The Woman of the Word

The Proverbs 31 description of the wife of a leader has encouraged me in this area. The Middle Eastern culture of her day was male dominated. Meaning, no doubt, she probably raised some eyebrows of those watching her serve her God, family and others. I'm certain she would have been seen as being a bit unconventional, which makes her my hero. Yet, as we read, notice that she did not allow the challenges to stop her from using her passions and gifts to be a special blessing to her family, others, and ultimately to her Lord.

> She selects wool and flax and works with eager hands.
>
> . . .
>
> She considers a field and buys it; out of her earnings she plants a vineyard.
>
> . . .
>
> She sees that her trading is profitable.
>
> . . .
>
> She opens her arms to the poor and extends her hands to the needy.
>
> . . .
>
> She makes linen garments and sells them, and supplies the merchants with sashes. (Proverbs 31:13, 16, 18a, 20, 24)

She is obviously an industrious woman with many passions and gifts that she used for the good of her family and the glory of God.

The Real-life Ministry World

Over the years God has allowed me the grace-filled freedom to pursue my gifts and passions for His glory. Some of my ministries would fall inside the box of normal church life for a pastor's wife. I have served in areas such as worship, Mothers of Pre-schoolers (M.O.P.S.), children's ministries, the nursery, women's ministries, and as church secretary. Then there are the ministries that are outside of the box, the eyebrow raisers. I'm sure you would like a little clarity, so here goes.

In our early years of ministry, I dedicated my life to

Terry and our two girls, definitely my passions. When the girls were preschoolers, I was a stay-at-home mom. Now, please understand that when we began ministry, we were as poor as church mice. Terry made $15,500 as a rookie youth pastor. We both did odd jobs on the side to help keep our household going. I cleaned houses and did some babysitting. Terry mowed yards and did side painting jobs for a little extra income. That is not a complaint. God taught us some important and valuable lessons in those days. We are thankful for his provision when we needed it the most. When the girls entered school, I once again entered the workforce and used my elementary teaching degree. We faced some mild opposition from those who thought I should stay at home, but we felt God was okay with our decision. I truly love to work, and for the next thirty years I remained part of the workforce. It was a decision our family made, and we believe there is much liberty and grace given in whatever decisions a pastor and his wife make in this area.

Another passion of mine is healthy living. I have always been a little bit of a hippie. In fact, Terry often gives me a hard time about my hippie ideas when it comes to being healthy. Years ago I fell in love with Young Living essential oils. If you talk to me for very long or add me as a friend on Facebook, Twitter, or Instagram, you will quickly see my love for essential oils. Now, if you're a skeptic and rolling your eyes, that is okay. Terry was skeptical at first as well; but as his health has increased and his doctor's visits decreased,

I finally won him over. In fact, one time, in a moment of weakness, he told me that if I could keep him healthy through a winter season, he would make a quick endorsement video with me. That winter he did the whole protocol I had laid out for him, and guess what? He stayed healthy. Since he is a man of his word, he did the Facebook video with me. Now that was fun. Here is the great thing. Not only are these products all natural and healthy, but this Young Living world is a whole new mission field for me. It allows me to rub shoulders consistently with people who are interested in healthy living, but many of them ultimately need a healing from the Great Physician, Jesus Christ. Another one of my passions, so another win-win.

My latest ministry giftedness and passion is for those in the sex industry. Yes, you read that correctly. I'm fairly confident you won't put this book down now. Here is my story. Several years ago Terry and I led a group from our church to Berlin, Germany, on a mission trip. While we were there, we were introduced to a women's ministry called The Alabaster Jar. The lady missionaries had created this ministry to reach into the lives of the sex-trafficked women of Berlin. In Germany, prostitution is a legalized business. Because of that, many women are illegally trafficked into Germany from neighboring countries. One night the ladies from our church were invited to go observe this ministry firsthand. All I can tell you is that it was heart wrenching! Young girls, the age of my young-adult daughters, were literally captives inside a foreign land with no way to return home. That evening as we walked the outskirts of those dark and hopeless streets, God began to put a heavy burden on my heart. I knew sex trafficking and the exploitation of women was not only happening in Berlin, Germany but also in the United States of America, and specifically in Indiana where we live.

When we returned home, I began to pray. The spark God placed in my heart in Germany began to develop into a flame. The burden never went away; it just continued to grow. I began doing research for ministries in the Indianapolis area that dealt with exploited women. I was convinced God would put me on the streets in Indianapolis like I had been on the streets in Berlin. I began to read books of sweet young girls who had been in the sex industry and by God's grace were miraculously rescued. I was surprised at the number of ministries around the country that focused specifically on this area of our culture. These books were like gasoline to the fire. I knew I had to keep pursuing this passion. Then, God did the unthinkable. Unbeknown to me, he had placed this same burden on the heart of another young woman in our church. In a random conversation one day this all came to light. God was moving and confirming the direction of our hearts.

After much prayer, counsel, and planning, we decided God did not want us to travel an hour to Indianapolis but rather start a ministry to the young women who worked at our local strip club, right here in Crawfordsville, Indiana. The goal was to take the light of Jesus Christ into the club in our community. The plan was to go in two times a month, go in with food and gifts, love on the girls, build bridges, speak the name of Jesus, give them Bibles, and tell them about the wonderful grace of an all-loving, compassionate, and forgiving Savior. The problem was that I am the wife of the pastor who leads the largest evangelical church in Montgomery county. What will people think? How will our church people respond? I think this may fall as far from a pastor's wife's job description as you can find. However, it's where God has placed my giftedness and passions, so there was no option. There was no turning back.

As we laid out the plan to the leadership of Rock Point Church, they were very supportive. It's one of the many reasons why I love our church. Their attitude, was, "go in and love on them in the name of Jesus!" And we did. Today we have a ministry called "Priceless" because these young women are priceless to a Savior who went to the cross on their behalf. We have the joy of sharing that good news with them. Our ministry has claimed these verses:

> The Spirit of the Lord is on me, because he has anointed me to proclaim good news to the poor. He has sent me to proclaim freedom for the prisoners and recovery of sight for the blind, to set the oppressed free, to proclaim the year of the Lord's favor. (Luke 4:18–19)

Now, ladies, think about the dilemma this was for my husband. He had to announce this new ministry to our church family. You see, in small town America there are no secrets. People find out everything, and I mean everything. At some point the local rumor mill would get started that the pastor's wife was going to the local strip club two times a month. What were our church people supposed to do with that rumor? On a Sunday morning Terry told our church family about this new ministry, and our people embraced it with a Christ-like enthusiasm.

There is so much more to this story. It's probably a book in and of itself. But let me say this, over the years we have been lovingly embraced by the owners, managers, and women of the club. They affectionately call us "the church ladies," one of my all-time favorite titles in this life. As you can imagine, we have some crazy stories of things that have happened over the years. We also have many God stories of ministering to these priceless women, seeing some of them visit our church services, and some coming to know Christ. It's a ministry of patience, perseverance, and prayer. God is faithful, and we love it!

If we lived according to the expectations of "that guy" that we talked about at the beginning of the chapter, I'm confident that "Priceless" would not be allowed in most churches. It's outside the box. It's not a traditional ministry for a church, and especially not for a pastor's wife. My calling is not to live according to the expectations of man but to live according to the gifts and passions that God has laid on my heart. One day when I stand before my God, I desire to hear, "Well done, good and faithful servant."

The Questions to Wrestle

1. As you have served as a pastor's wife, what expectations have you felt from your churches? Where did those expectations come from?
2. If your current church had a job description for the pastor's wife, what would it look like?
3. How much of a struggle is people pleasing to you? Why?
4. What are some areas of life that you enjoy, areas where your passions and giftedness intersect? Do you serve in those areas?
5. Are there any areas of service you are fearful to pursue because of expectations? What would you pursue if given the green light? What are some next steps to beginning that journey?

CHAPTER 5

HIS BATTLES

The Dodgeball Warriors – "The Medic"

Who would have thought that the simple game of dodgeball, with almost no rules, would have so many interesting facets that apply to life and ministry? Even though it is total chaos, everyone eventually seems to find a role within the game. Some are the "dodgers."

They hang in the back and use all of their evasive skills to stay alive as long as possible. Others are the "ballers." They are the front-line maniacs who charge the enemy lines with reckless abandon. It's the wisdom of the dodgers that usually finds them making it to the final standoff. There is another group that is often overlooked. I call them the "medics." Inevitably, during the game someone will take that nasty blow to the head and stagger to the sidelines. The gym teacher usually just smirks as the wounded warrior heads to the bleachers to have a seat. The teacher's attitude is, "That will toughen him up, and he needed it."

Every team also had the "medic." The medic was the person who would tend to the needs of the wounded warrior. They were the compassionate souls who would move to the end of the bench to comfort and lend assistance. It was not their personality to charge the floor and confront the enemy in defense of their teammate who just got hurt. They simply stayed behind the battle lines to love and support the incoming wounded.

I didn't realize one of the roles I would be playing as a pastor's wife would be that of the medic. It is so mission critical to the success of the team that it cannot be overlooked.

His Battles

Before I address the topic of "his battles" and the spiritual-warfare battles a pastor often faces, please allow me to make a few comments. Terry and I have loved our lifetime calling to full-time ministry. God has given us so many blessings, far too numerous to count. We have served with some amazingly talented people. We have made lifelong friendships. In every place where we have served, we found people who lovingly adopted us as part of their families. Ministry often relocates a pastor's family away from their biological families, so these homes were a special blessing to us every time. Looking back, we would not choose any other way to spend our lives other than serving Christ full-time. We have been blessed and fulfilled in his calling on our lives. As I talk about "his battles," please do not read this as, "Poor me, we are victims, ministry stinks, don't go into ministry, we have had a terrible life." Nothing could be further from the truth. In every life there are always good things as well challenges. The challenges can be difficult, but God has always used them to grow us and prepare us for the next season of ministry. So, here we go, charging the front lines of the battlefield!

The Real-life Ministry World

Every pastor's wife should be required to have "medical" training because, in this very real spiritual battle of life and ministry, there will be wounded warriors who need help. Many times the front-line person needing assistance, who just took that nasty blow to the head, will be your husband. As the leader of the troops, he is not only on the front lines daily, but he also wears the biggest target on his back. When there is warfare, he is called to lead the charge into the heart of the battle. It's part of his duty and because of that, there are times he will come staggering home in need of a loving medic at his side.

In these days of battle a pastor's wife needs to carefully play her role as a medic and resist the urge to charge the floor and confront the enemy in defense of her wounded teammate. It is not the calling of the pastor's wife to fight her husband's battles for him. It is her calling to make sure he can remain on the front lines to lead his team. It is her job to prayerfully patch him up and send him back inspired for the next day.

Since 1985 I have seen Terry lead the troops into many various types of battles. Some are more like skirmishes. They are relatively short, not extremely intense, and create small bumps and bruises that mend quickly. However, others are much more intense; the duration is long, and the wounds are deep, which then turns our home into the proverbial ER room of the hospital.

Here are a few examples in which I have witnessed Terry stand strong in the midst of turbulent waters and trying times. If you're a pastor's wife, I know you can relate.

The Fallen Shepherd

In our first ministry the long-tenured, lead pastor we served under had to step down because of severe financial, family, and ministry integrity issues. As you can imagine, that rocked our church to the foundation. The aftershocks literally lasted for years. As a young youth pastor, Terry was called to the front lines to lead. He will be the first one to admit that he didn't do it perfectly; no one ever does in a prolonged situation where sin has had such a devastating impact. There were endless meetings and endless issues to be resolved. The full story is far too long and complex for this segment, but here is what I remember: many nights of him falling asleep with tears staining his pillowcase. In those days he didn't need an armor-bearer to grab a sword and attack the enemy; he needed a medic. That was my role. Day after day I lovingly and prayerfully patched him up and sent him back to the front lines.

The Pedophile

I have seen Terry stand before TV news cameras and address the heart-wrenching issue of a pedophile who infiltrated our church. This predator carefully passed all of our church's background checks and security protocols. When the situation came to light and the allegations were finally confirmed, it was unimaginable that this was happening in our church. Terry and another one of our pastors met this individual and confronted him with the evidence. As he confessed, they cried together and prayed together; then they escorted him to the police station to turn himself over to the authorities. As the news broke in our community, it was mass chaos for about forty-eight hours. Our church was wisely instructed by counsel to have one spokesperson to address the media and do all the interviews. That was my husband. Our church took some of those major dodgeball blows to the head over this situation. Social media was an opportunistic platform for all who were looking for a chance to shoot the fiery arrows. The leader, the spokesman, the man wearing the biggest target on his back took the most hits for the team. When it's your husband leading through the midst of that battle, trust me, your home will be his ER when he arrives home from those days.

Unexpected Home Going

On a fateful morning in January, one of our dear pastoral staff members, a forty-two-year-old, healthy, happily married man with two young boys, was suddenly called home to heaven. This particular morning, he had been playing basketball with some men at a local church. As he left, he had a sudden heart attack and didn't make it through the day. Terry and I were at the hospital when the doctor gave the devastating news to his young wife. We then were at their home when she told her two boys the heartbreaking news. The depth of their sorrow in that moment is impossible to describe. I witnessed an emotional pain throughout our church family unlike anything I had seen in our twenty-plus years. Once again, it was Terry called to the front line to lead our church through those days and preach the celebration of life service for his dear friend.

Building Program

If you want to talk about an intense game of dodgeball, watch the toll it takes on your husband when he attempts to lead the church through a multi-million-dollar building program. To compound our situation, it was also a site relocation and church name change all at the same time. In those chaotic days, many people left the church because of fear of the commitment needed to move forward. Others complained about the selected builder and design plans. That list goes on and on. Terry personally felt every attack because each one threatened the unity of Christ's church. I specifically remember the weight on him being the church representative that signed the $3.8 million construction loan as we began the project. This was all happening in 2008 when our country experienced one of the worst economic downturns in its history. For a man who had kept our church debt free and hates debt, this caused him many sleepless nights. There aren't many things that have the potential to cause extreme chaos within a church, but a building project is one of those things. Praise God we all made it! Thankfully, the years following that endeavor have been filled with God's blessings.

Church Discipline

Leading through sin issues in a church is exceptionally draining on a pastor. When Terry has to lead the church family through a church-discipline issue, it takes an emotional drain on him unlike almost anything else. On top of that stress, there is always the blowback from the community about how Rock Point Church hates people and kicks them out of the church. It's another opportunity for people to zero in on the man wearing the biggest target and take a shot.

Removal of Staff

When Terry leads in the decision to let a staff member go, it wounds him deeply. These people have been a part of the staff family. They are friends. Their livelihood and family will potentially be impacted greatly, and he knows it. Even though it is ultimately the best decision for the future of the church, it's still never an easy process. It's a heavy weight for him to carry every time.

Leadership Struggles

Friendly fire, as they call it in warfare, probably wounds him the most. King David talks about this kind of hurt.

> Destructive forces are at work in the city; threats and lies never leave its streets. If an enemy were insulting me, I could endure it; if a foe were rising against me, I could hide. But it is you, a man like myself, my companion, my close friend, with whom I once enjoyed sweet fellowship at the house of God, as we walked about among the worshipers. (Psalm 55:11–14)

> Even my close friend, someone I trusted, one who shared my bread, has turned against me. (Psalm 41:9)

Our church has had an incredible stretch of unity both among the leadership team and the church family. We have been very blessed, but there are always occasions when things get a little dicey within the leadership circle. When those moments arrive, I can see how it takes some of the sparkle from his smile.

Rumors

Church rumors always reflect on the leader. In our community, there has been a rumor for years that if you join Rock Point Church you have to submit your W-2 so that the church can make sure all of its members are tithing. I know! It's ludicrous! Welcome to small town America. Those nagging rumors are like a little dog that continuously nips at his heels. They are aggravating to Terry, and they seemingly never go away.

Burnout

Over time, ministry takes a toll. It is very real physical and spiritual warfare. No matter how hard you try, or how diligently you plan, sometimes the exhaustion catches up. When Terry is running on fumes after lengthy seasons of ministry life, I will see its effect at home, even if people don't see it on Sundays. It's my duty to encourage him and keep him going until the next break appears on the calendar.

Those are his battles. Those are the battles where pastors are called to lead. You as a pastor's wife know all too well about his battles. You have lived through them with him. You know the pain. You feel the tension. You desire to help. That is what wives do. Yet, one of the most challenging things for us is that even though we are in the heat of the battle with our man, we are not called to step in and fight his battles for him. In fact, if we make the decision to charge the floor and confront the enemy, it will actually compound his problems and add more stress. Trust me, it will not make things better. He does not need us engaging in the battle. He needs us engaging him when he arrives home exhausted from the battle. He needs a medic.

The Woman of the Word

As I referenced earlier in the book, I am struck that the husband in Proverbs 31 is the man who sits at the city gate. In ancient times this is where the leaders conducted the business of the city. This is where disputes were handled. This is where heated arguments happened. This was a place of personal battles between those leading the city. I've noticed that the wife of this leader did not engage in the area that was his turf, his battleground. She had her things that she did with extreme care, but entering his arena is not one that is listed. In her wisdom of carefully understanding her role, she is then praised at the city gate:

> Honor her for all that her hands have done, and let her works bring her praise at the city gate. (Proverbs 31:31)

His Battles/My Battles

As a pastor's wife, his battles do, in a real sense, become my battles as well. I hear about them, I give counsel, I pray for him, I patch him up as a loving medic so he can face another day. But my battle is real in a different way. Eventually I will come face-to-face with some of the people from the battlefield, some of the people that may have been inflicting injury to my man. I know the people personally. I know the insider stories. I have an opinion. I have feelings. I have something to say. Every part of me wants to jump in and defend. But I can't. I must not fight his battles for him. I must pray for *grace*! I must continue to love. I must continue to smile. I must be the Proverbs 31 wife of a leader who "brings him good and not harm all the days of his life." Bringing him good means living with a Christlike attitude in the midst of the emotion. It means representing my Savior before representing myself. Yes, it's challenging, but I must remind myself that patience, self-control, and grace are badges of honor. If I can humbly display them in situations like this, it represents major victories for the team.

> Patience is better than power, and controlling one's emotions, than capturing a city. (Proverbs 16:32 CSB)

> A gracious woman gains honor. (Proverbs 11:16a)

I must remember that, in his battles, he needs me to be the gracious, loving medic, not the protective armor-bearer engaging the enemy. I must also remember that in my battles within his battles, God's grace is sufficient to give me the strength needed.

> But he said to me, "My grace is sufficient for you, for my power is made perfect in weakness." Therefore I will boast all the more gladly about my weaknesses, so that Christ's power may rest on me. (2 Corinthians 2:9)

The Questions to Wrestle

1. How well do you function as the team medic? What are some effective ways you refresh your husband when he comes home from the heat of the battle?
2. Share a couple of your pastor-husband's battles that you have witnessed firsthand. What was the hardest part for him? What was the hardest part for you?
3. Are there times you have decided to be the armor bearer and enter the battle? Please share. What was the outcome? Did it make the situation better or worse? If you were to do it over again, what would you do differently?
4. In the midst of his battles, what are some ways you keep your emotions in check and exercise *grace* to others?
5. How has God grown you through the ministry battles you have faced?

CHAPTER 6

OUR DISCOURAGEMENTS

Dodgeball: "Defeat"

"The thrill of victory and the agony of defeat" is the old phrase from the introduction to ABC's *Wide World of Sports*. It's a phrase that correctly describes the final result of any competition or battle. Ultimately, someone wins, and someone loses. At the conclusion of each dodgeball game, there are just two people left standing, one from each team. It's win or lose. It's either walk off the floor as the team's hero or as the team's failure. There is a lot on the line, or at least it seemed like it during those middle school years. In any team sport, if you are the last one standing, you represent the team. If you win, everyone gives you a high five. If you lose, everyone feels the hurt and disappointment of not being one of the champions of that day. Winning and celebration are very much a team dynamic, and so are losing and discouragement. Everyone loves to be a winner, and everyone hates to be the loser. This can easily be substantiated because I have yet to find anyone whose goal in life is to continually be on the losing side of the scoreboard. To the victors go the spoils, and I might add, the bragging rights. In middle school, bragging rights are a highly valued commodity.

Our Discouragements

Ministry life is a small microcosm of life as a whole. There are many good days of blessings and rejoicing, and by God's grace there are fewer difficult days of defeat and discouragement. But those challenging days can bring much pain and heartache. We see this in the life of many women in the Bible.

I'm confident Eve's heart felt immense pain and discouragement when the news arrived that her first-born son, Cain, had taken the life of her second-born son, Abel. The love of a mom for her children is virtually impossible to put into words. All of us moms know this to be true: once a mom, always a mom. It doesn't matter how old our children get, when they hurt, we hurt. We are not told of Eve's reaction to the news of this murder, but we do get a glimpse of her heart with the birth of her next son, Seth:

> Adam made love to his wife again, and she gave birth to a son and named him Seth, saying, 'God has granted me another child in place of Abel, since Cain killed him.' (Genesis 4:25)

Hannah faced the pain and discouragement of not being able to have children for the majority of her life.

> In her deep anguish Hannah prayed to the Lord, weeping bitterly. And she made a vow, saying, "Lord Almighty, if you will only look on your servant's misery and remember me, and not forget your servant but give her a son, then I will give him to the Lord for all the days of his life, and no razor will ever be used on his head." (1 Samuel 1:10–11)

Mary must have experienced a broken heart as she witnessed the crucifixion of her son, the Lord Jesus Christ. As a mother, I can't even begin to imagine the immense pain Mary endured as she stood near the cross. To personally witness the agony, suffering, and eventual death of her son had to be almost unbearable.

> Near the cross of Jesus stood his mother, his mother's sister, Mary the wife of Clopas, and Mary Magdalene. When Jesus saw his mother there, and the disciple whom he loved standing nearby, he said to her, "Woman, here is your son," and to the disciple, "Here is your mother." From that time on, this disciple took her into his home. (John 19:25–27)

Pain and discouragement are real. They are part of life. They are part of living in a sin-cursed world. Christ reminded his disciples of this very fact:

> I have told you these things, so that in me you may have peace. In this world you will have trouble. But take heart! I have overcome the world. (John 16:33)

If you, as a wife, find yourself in ministry, then be assured of this: in this world you will have trouble. You will face defeat, failure, and discouragement. But take heart! You are not in this alone. Not only is Christ on your side, but you are also part of a team. You have a companion. You have a partner and a friend. The lovesick woman in the Song of Solomon said it this way,

> His mouth is sweetness itself; he is altogether lovely. This is my beloved, this is my friend, daughters of Jerusalem. (Song of Solomon 5:16)

You have been blessed with someone to do life and ministry with you. You have a husband, a friend, and you need each other. Be assured that on a healthy team there will always be someone with you that will always have your back. Attempting to do ministry apart from a strong united front would be unbearable. So, ladies, how's your marriage? How's your team? How are you doing?

In an earlier chapter I mentioned the importance of being a healthy wife. We all know the phrase, "happy wife, happy life." And we all know there is much more truth to that statement than we care to admit. So, let's talk health for a minute before we talk about how to stay united as a team to work through discouragements.

The Woman of the Word

Proverbs 31 seems to paint a picture of a perfect wife, marriage, and family. In reality, we know there is no such thing. I love Hallmark Christmas movies. They are some of my favorite things to watch in December. Why? Because who doesn't like a good ending and a happily-ever-after at the end of each episode? In the midst of this chaotic, depressing world, give me the feel-good, happily-ever-after every day and all day long. Now, Terry likes to bring the rain clouds to my happy place. He always makes his sarcastic comments about "not being able to figure out the plot and how it is going to end." Then I remind him that sarcasm is not a spiritual gift. But seriously, what if things in life always ended perfectly? Someday in heaven they will, but we are not there yet and neither was the Proverbs 31 woman. Here is what we do know: the life of this wife was not perfect. The text clearly says it:

> Her children arise and call her blessed; her husband also, and he praises her. (Proverbs 31:28)

How do we know her life was not perfect? She had kids and a husband. Enough said. Drop the mic and walk off the stage.

When life is not perfect, we will face discouragements. How do we handle them? Let's be honest. We all live in a real world with real problems. Here is what I would like us to see from Proverbs 31:

> She draws on her strength and reveals that her arms are strong. (Proverbs 31:17 CSB)

This wife of a leader was strong. The text indicates she was healthy. This is so important to take note of for this reason. When we face discouragements, being in a good, healthy place in our lives is vital. It allows us to work through the discouragements without being completely overwhelmed. Let's take a look at some helpful thoughts about being a healthy pastor's wife.

The Real-life Ministry World

At Small Church USA, we help churches diagnose five main areas that affect church health. Two of these areas are the health of the pastor and the health of his wife. When we say health, we are referring to the physical, emotional, and spiritual well-being of the individual. We believe the health of both the pastor and his wife are critically important for a thriving church. Over the years we have heard far too many stories of marital issues that eventually led to a couple leaving the ministry.

Here is a quick snapshot of our philosophy at Small Church USA. We believe God's Word that the church is a body, a living organism.

> He is before all things, and in him all things hold together. And he is the head of the body, the church; he is the beginning

> and the firstborn from among the dead, so that in everything he might have the supremacy. (Colossians 1:17–18)

Using Paul's analogy of the church being a body, we believe it is critical to identify the vital, internal organs of the church body. If the life-giving internal organs are healthy, it will ensure the body is functioning at its maximum capacity.

The study of anatomy reveals that the human body has five vital internal organs: brain, heart, lungs, kidneys, and liver. If any of these organs are unhealthy, the body will be unhealthy. If any of these organs are not working in complete conjunction with each other, the body will be unhealthy. We believe the church has five internal vital organs as well. I will not take time to explain all of the five, but I will address two.[1]

First, we like to correlate the pastor with being the heart of the church. He pumps the life blood into the body. He sets the culture, the atmosphere, the pace, the energy, the attitude, and the direction, just to mention a few. If the heart is not healthy, certainly the church will not be healthy. Heart attacks can be fatal.

Second, we correlate the pastor's wife to the lungs. Here is what the American Heart Association says about the vital role the heart and the lungs play within the body: "the heart and the lungs work together to produce oxygen-rich blood to the body."

The lungs play this key role: They take the

1 For a more comprehensive discussion on this topic, please visit our web site at: smallchurchusa.com.

oxygen-depleted blood and infuse it with oxygen. This newly refreshed blood is first sent to the heart to keep the heart healthy, and then the heart pumps the oxygen-rich blood to the rest of the body. I'm sure you can see the importance of the imagery. Without the heart and lungs working together, the body cannot be healthy. Likewise, without the pastor and his wife working together, the church body cannot be healthy.

We firmly believe that the pastor's wife plays a critical role in the life of her husband and, therefore, the church. If a pastor's wife is unhealthy and not growing, it will eventually take a toll on the pastor. The heart and lungs must be healthy and work together. If proper care is given to ensure the health of the wife, we believe that pays many dividends.

Eve was the first woman, wife, and mother. Her name in the Hebrew language is significant. It means, "to give life or to breathe life into." Women, wives, and moms are life-givers. It's what we do. It's what our name means. We are called to continually give to the team. We give affection, support, love, care, tenderness, and inspiration. We wear many hats: chef, counselor, taxi driver, cleaner, tutor, sanitary engineer, nurse, referee, personal assistant, teacher, classroom assistant, accountant, entertainer, investigator, translator, dental hygienist, researcher, travel agent, personal trainer, and bargain hunter. It is a life of blessing by giving to others, and it's how all Christ followers should strive to live.

> In everything I did, I showed you that by this kind of hard work we must help the weak, remembering the words the Lord Jesus himself said: "It is more blessed to give than to receive. (Acts 20:35)

> Do nothing out of selfish ambition or vain conceit. Rather, in humility value others above yourselves, not looking to your own interests but each of you to the interests of the others. (Philippians 2:3–4)

But let's be honest, being a life-giver can be exhausting. There are times when the lungs need to take in oxygen as they continually provide needed oxygen to others.

Every time I board an airplane I am reminded of this truth. As people find their seats and get settled, the flight attendants always begin with the safety briefing. Part of this preflight briefing addresses what will happen in the event of an emergency. If you have flown as many times as we have, I'm sure you can probably quote this almost verbatim.

> Ladies and gentlemen, on behalf of the crew I ask that you please direct your attention to the monitors above as we review the emergency procedures. There are six emergency exits on this aircraft. Take a minute to locate the exit closest to you. Note that the nearest exit may be behind you. Count the number of rows to this exit. Should the cabin experience sudden pressure loss, stay calm and listen for instructions from the cabin crew. Oxygen masks

> will drop down from above your seat. Place the mask over your mouth and nose, like this. Pull the strap to tighten it. If you are traveling with children, make sure that your own mask is on first before helping your children.

Their directions are clear as to the protocol in the unlikely event of an emergency. They instruct you to put your oxygen mask on first, then assist those who may be traveling with you. That may not seem like "thinking of others before thinking of myself," but their point is well made. If you, as the responsible, life-giving adult, have a lack of oxygen that renders you weak and unhealthy, you will be of no help to those around you. Weak and unhealthy people do not help others gain strength and vitality.

We believe many pastors' wives have ignored their oxygen mask to the detriment of their husband and families. So, ladies, what does it look like to put on the oxygen mask? What kinds of things can you implement into your lives to make sure you are healthy and functioning at a high level? Here is a brief look at the five areas we believe will give a pastor's wife the refreshing oxygen she so desperately needs. They are in the acrostic of L.U.N.G.S.

L – Life Giving

What areas of your life are life-giving to you? What things do you intentionally build into your life that pump fresh, clean oxygen into your soul? If you are going to be an oxygen giver, you must make sure your lungs are continually being filled as well. Here are a few of my life-giving favorites.

I am a beach and water girl. I grew up in "Pure Michigan," as the slogan says, a state where lakes are in abundance. I love the sand and the sun. Today, put me on a beach chair with an ocean breeze, blue skies, and a book in my hand, and that is pure oxygen to my soul.

I also need alone time with Terry. Now that we are empty nesters, it is much easier to get away together. But even when our kids were at home we always tried to make it a priority to find "us time" in the midst of the chaos.

Making time to exercise is another area that gives me oxygen. When I neglect this area of my life it takes a toll on how I feel and how I perform.

What are your ways of recharging that bring life? You need to identify them and make them a priority. Seriously, it's not about you being selfish; it's about you being your best for others. Put your oxygen mask on first.

U – Unapologetically You

We covered this in an earlier chapter, but let me address it again. Please do not attempt to live according to the expectations of others. Be you. Be the person God created you to be. Do the good works God created you to do. Find the place where your passions and gifts intersect and serve in those areas. It will be life giving to your soul. Be the very best workmanship you can be to the glory of God.

N – Nurturing Friendships

We all need friends. In all honesty, because of the nature of church-ministry life, we probably won't have a bus full of them. But we all need a few. Over the years I have had a small group of ladies who are near and dear to my life. They are the needed oxygen for my soul. They have played such an important role in my life. They love Jesus deeply. I trust them. They are airtight when it comes to confidences. We laugh together, cry together, pray together, and stay in touch regularly with each other. I cannot imagine trying to navigate the waters of ministry without their support.

G – Grace

Simply stated, we need to give ourselves grace and we need to learn to extend grace to those around us. Both sides of this coin are equally important. Let's be honest, vulnerable, and authentic; and say it like it is. We ladies have issues. As my husband would often lovingly say to our church family, "All of us are just a bunch of dirty rotten sinners." Thankfully, we are sinners miraculously saved by God's amazing grace.

> Or do you not know that the unrighteous will not inherit the kingdom of God? Do not be deceived: neither the sexually immoral, nor idolaters, nor adulterers, nor men who practice homosexuality, nor thieves, nor the greedy, nor drunkards, nor revilers, nor swindlers will inherit the kingdom of God. And such were some of you. But you were washed, you were sanctified, you were justified in the name of the Lord Jesus Christ and by the Spirit of our God. (1 Corinthians 6:9–11)

Praise God for his forgiveness and grace! But truth be told, we are probably harder on ourselves than grace would allow us to be. Most of the ladies I talk with have several areas where they need to liberally apply more grace. I have those areas as well. Some of us, if not all of us, have "our story," something from our past that we would like to bury in the deepest hole we can find and never see again, but there doesn't seem to be a hole deep enough. Because of some of these events, we may face things such as insecurities, the strain of inadequacies, the feeling of being unworthy, we don't trust, we are shackled, we are prisoners of our past. These areas quickly become strongholds in our lives. We must apply grace! We must take every thought captive to Christ.

> For though we live in the world, we do not wage war as the world does. The weapons we fight with are not the

> weapons of the world. On the contrary, they have divine power to demolish strongholds. We demolish arguments and every pretension that sets itself up against the knowledge of God, and we take captive every thought to make it obedient to Christ. (2 Corinthians 10:3–5)

There is probably an endless list of areas where we try to be someone other than who God created us to be. We try to compensate for our past. We need grace! We need to apply it liberally to all of those challenging areas. Our past and "our story" need to be placed under the grace of God's abiding love. If it is not put there, it will quickly suck the oxygen out of our lives and cause us to be unhealthy.

We also need to extend grace to others. A grace-filled pastor's wife is also a wife who will bring her husband good and not harm all the days of his life. Grace helps us love the unlovely. Grace attracts friendships. Grace puts a smile on our faces. Grace mends hurts. Grace brightens the day. Grace provides oxygen to our souls. As Paul says,

> Let your conversation be always full of grace, seasoned with salt, so that you may know how to answer everyone. (Colossians 4:6)

S - Seasons

Life has many seasons. I have personally journeyed through many of them. Single, married without kids, married with kids, all of the seasons of having kids (toddlers, preschool, grade school, middle school, high school, college), then came weddings and being an empty nester, and then the best season, Grammy to our grandkids.

One of the challenging things about seasons is that they are all different. As Solomon reminds us,

> There is a time for everything, and a season for every activity under the heavens. (Ecclesiastes 3:1)

All seasons have different requirements related to what and how much you give. Some seasons of life may require the minimal amount of oxygen intake that comes from breathing normally. Other seasons will require the full-on face mask and oxygen tank hooked to the pull-behind cart. It's important to understand the season and make the needed adjustments for the proper intake of oxygen.

Paul said to the young pastor Timothy,

> Watch your life and doctrine closely. Persevere in them, because if you do, you will save both yourself and your hearers. (1 Timothy 4:16)

I think we could safely say that Paul's admonition to Timothy was to put on your oxygen mask first. Take care of yourself. Keep yourself healthy. If you are not healthy, you cannot help others.

How does being mindful of our health play into our discouragements? Discouragements are much more manageable when we are healthy. Discouragements are more easily faced when our marriages are strong. Discouragements don't overwhelm us as easily when life is not already overwhelming.

In 2020 the world faced an unexpected pandemic. The COVID-19 virus literally brought our world and our country to a screeching halt in a matter of weeks. It was something unlike any of our generation had ever seen. As we all tried to stay healthy, social distance, and survive this potentially life-threating virus, there was one common warning. If your health is already compromised, you must take extreme precautions. The people groups most at risk were those who already had underlying health issues. For many of the unhealthy in our world, this became a death sentence as it claimed hundreds of thousands of lives.

The lesson is easily applied. The better health we can maintain, the better we can handle the challenges of life. We will win some and lose some. No one is ever on the winning team all the time, but the better we maintain our health, the more valuable we will be to the team. Remember, our teammates are counting on us to do our part.

The Questions to Wrestle

1. What are some areas of life and ministry that get you discouraged? What affect does that have on you? What affect does that have on your husband?

Let's talk L.U.N.G.S.

2. Life Giving. Share one or two activities that are life giving to you? How often do you prioritize them into your schedule?
3. Unapologetically You. Questions about this topic were covered in chapter 4, but just a reminder, be you!
4. Nurturing Friendships. Do you have close trusted friends? If not, why? If yes, how did you cultivate those friendships?
5. Grace. In what areas of life do you need to exercise more grace to yourself? Would people say you are a grace giver? If not, what are some ways to grow in this area?
6. Seasons. What is your current season of life? Are you managing it well? What needs to change in order to make this season more life giving to you?

CHAPTER 7

OUR FAMILY

Dodgeball Warriors: "The Underdog"

Every team has the underdog, the person who seemingly just isn't as athletic, or skilled, or brave, or coordinated as the rest. They usually are the first target for the other team to put in its crosshairs because they are the easy out. This person generally doesn't resist much or even attempt to avoid the incoming balls. It's usually painful and sad to watch, game after game, as they get eliminated and sit the rest of the time, content to simply watch.

Occasionally someone on the team has the brilliant idea of protecting the underdog in hopes of making them feel as if they are part of the team and a valuable asset, which of course they are. On a true team, every team member has value. When this happens, the team rallies together for a common cause, which generally brings out the best in any team. If they are successful in their protection scheme, and the longer the plan works, the more the excitement grows. Even when one of the top players on the team is eliminated, it is often seen as a victory because of the greater cause. It is not uncommon to see the eliminated "A" team players standing and cheering from the bench as the team fights for the victory of protecting the underdog. It's in those games that a true sense of accomplishment is felt by all. No one is left out. Everyone is pulling the same direction. All are shown value. Sacrifice is seen as a badge of honor, and a group of selfish individuals has now become a family. They have been transformed into people who care for, cheer for, and protect one another. It's a beautiful thing to behold.

The Woman of the Word

The Proverbs 31 woman was not only the wife of a leader, she was also blessed to be a mom of several children:

> Her children arise and call her blessed; her husband also, and he praises her. (Proverbs 31:28)

That means she was part of a family. That means she was in the long line of women who were the ultimate multitaskers. She was a wearer of many hats, a juggler of numerous double-edged knives all at one time, a hub for all of the spokes of the household wheel, an operations director at command central. Just read the text; she was a vital part of the family and much needed.

> She gets up while it is still night; she provides food for her family. . . . When it snows, she has no fear for her household; for all of them are clothed in scarlet. . . . She speaks with wisdom, and faithful instruction is on her tongue. She watches over the affairs of her household and does not eat the bread of idleness. (Proverbs 31:15, 21, 26–27)

As with any family, we should never refer to our tribe as "my family" but as "our family." Let's address some areas where we can help our family thrive in the midst of the chaos of ministry.

The Real-life Ministry World

Ministry life is an interesting dynamic for families. We have talked about some of the unique challenges for pastors and wives, so let me say a word about our children. They are on the team too. They have a unique role to play and can often feel like the underdogs of the team in some situations.

We have two wonderful girls. They maneuvered through the landmines of being teenagers while living in small town America as PK's (pastor's kids). And yes, they hit a few landmines along the way like all kids do. Their family life is also a bit unique and one that most others won't completely understand. They at times feel an extra weight of pressure because their dad is a local pastor. There are probably a few more sets of eyes focused on them than on other kids. There could be some unrealistic expectations that others put on them. Their failures may get more attention. There may even be some in the community who desire to see them trip up and fall. Remember, it's not a dodgeball game; it's real life, real battles, real enemy, and real family. As Peter says,

> Be sober-minded, be alert. Your adversary the devil is prowling around like a roaring lion, looking for anyone he can devour .(1 Peter 5:8)

Pastors' kids, like many of the children of prominent Bible characters, will struggle and fail. Serving God full-time does not come with an invisible force field of safety from real-life temptations and our sinful hearts. Look at what God's Word says about the families of some of the most renowned prophets, patriarchs, priests, and recognized people from the nation of Israel.

> Eli's sons: "Eli's sons were scoundrels; they had no regard for the Lord. . . . This sin of the young men was very great in the Lord's sight, for they were treating the Lord's offering with contempt." (1 Samuel 2:12, 17)

> Joseph's brothers: "Judah said to his brothers, 'What do we gain if we kill our brother and cover up his blood? Come on, let's sell him to the Ishmaelites and not lay a hand on him, for he is our brother, our own flesh,' and his brothers agreed. When Midianite traders passed by, his brothers pulled Joseph out of the pit and sold him for twenty pieces

> of silver to the Ishmaelites, who took Joseph to Egypt." (Genesis 37:26–28)
>
> Lot's daughters: "The next day the firstborn said to the younger, 'Look, I slept with my father last night. Let's get him to drink wine again tonight so you can go sleep with him and we can preserve our father's line.' That night they again got their father to drink wine, and the younger went and slept with him; he did not know when she lay down or when she got up." (Genesis 19:34-35)
>
> King David's son: "'Bring the meal to the bedroom,' Amnon told Tamar, 'so I can eat from your hand.' Tamar took the cakes she had made and went to her brother Amnon's bedroom. When she brought them to him to eat, he grabbed her and said, 'Come sleep with me, my sister!'
> 'Don't, my brother!' she cried. 'Don't disgrace me, for such a thing should never be done in Israel. Don't commit this outrage! Where could I ever go with my humiliation? And you—you would be like one of the outrageous fools in Israel! Please, speak to the king, for he won't keep me from you.' But he refused to listen to her, and because he was stronger than she was, he disgraced her by raping her." (2 Samuel 13:10–14)

All families have struggles. Our lives are real like everyone else's. To pretend that our families are different is simply not true. To put on a facade that we have it all together is dangerous. We must not deceive or be hypocritical in this area. When ministry kids mess up, people in town talk. Juicy gossip spreads quickly. People in our churches are not naive. They know. So let's be real families that have to work through real issues just like everyone else.

Through the thick and thin, our families must be committed to staying together and supporting each other. When one falls we must be there for them. We rally to the wounded teammate to surround them with love, provide godly counsel, and help get them back on their feet. It's in these challenging days that they need the team more than ever.

> Two are better than one, because they have a good return for their labor: If either of them falls down, one can help the other up. But pity anyone who falls and has no one to help them up. Also, if two lie down together, they will keep warm. But how can one keep warm alone? Though one may be overpowered, two can defend themselves. A cord of three strands is not quickly broken. (Ecclesiastes 4:9–12)

Pastors' families are no different than regular families. In fact, there is a little more on the line for pastor's families according to the qualifications of 1 Timothy 3. In essence, it states that if a pastor loses his family, he will also lose his ministry. Yes. That places a higher demand on pastors and their families.

> He must manage his own family well and see that his children obey him, and he must do so in a manner worthy of full respect. (If anyone does not know how to manage

> his own family, how can he take care of God's church?) (1 Timothy 3:4–5)

Here are four areas where our families can rally together to support one another. Moms will play a key role in all of these areas, so let's be diligent to pray for wisdom and guidance. If you're like me, I will take all I can get! My family means the world to me. Proverbs states,

> The wise woman builds her house, but with her own hands the foolish one tears hers down. (Proverbs 14:1)

Oh Lord, please fill me with your wisdom! I want to be a builder of my home, not one that causes damage.

So what does it take to be a successful builder of children when it comes to helping them grow in the training and instruction of the Lord?

If you have ever watched the Disney classic *Mary Poppins*, then you will remember the multicolored nanny bag that Mary always carried with her. She never left home without it. This special bag always seemed to contain exactly what was needed to ensure the children learned the valuable life lessons of the moment. As moms we also need our figurative Mary Poppins bag with us at all times. What essentials do we need in our bag? I would suggest pom-poms, a whistle, a red pen, and a first-aid kit. Does that sound reasonable? If so, let's take a look at why these are necessities.

Cheerleader

Grab the pom-poms because everyone loves to be cheered on by others. Everyone loves being on a team where there is an abundance of encouragement and enthusiasm. Having fun with the family cannot be overstated. In 2020 the Covid-19 pandemic literally crippled our world. Families were to stay quarantined and isolated as much as possible. There were no sporting events, no malls were open, parks were closed, movie theaters shut down, restaurants only had drive-through service, the school year was suspended, and all non-essential activities were forbidden. These were unparalleled days in our lifetime. But it forced families to actually be families again. Families had to eat together, play together, work together, and have family social interaction. It re-created families into "our" family again. I heard so many great stories of families playing together and laughing together. What a blessing it is to have fun. It should be a staple in our homes:

> A cheerful heart is good medicine, but a crushed spirit dries up the bones. (Proverbs 17:22)

Families need to be each other's biggest cheerleaders. One of my favorite sayings is this: "Say yes to your kids as much as you can." If it's not sinful, disrespectful, or harmful, "yes" wins the day. This is not to say we enable our children and give them everything they want. There always needs to be a balance. However, when it comes to parenting it is easy to get into the habit of "Just say no." Many times, for me, there really wasn't a great reason; it's just the first thing to come out of my mouth. I'm not sure why.

When our girls were in high school, we would occasionally get this question from them on a weekend, "Hey Mom and Dad, can our friends spend the night Friday?" Then the follow up question, "and will you take us TP-ing? We want to get so-and-so's house." The answer? Yes! However, part of the deal was, they had to supply their own rolls of toilet paper (TP) that was going to end up being the masterpiece in their friend's trees. Not only did we give an enthusiastic "Yes," but Terry would camo them up in his hunting gear and face paint. We would then be the designated getaway driver if a quick escape was needed. Yes, we even threw a few rolls of TP as well. What fun is TP-ing with your kids if you are not in on the action? I mean, it's discipleship at its finest, the older teaching the younger. We still reminisce and laugh about those TP-ing exploits. Such great memories! We hope we can teach the next generation of grandkids as well. Oh, and by the way, they had to supply their own TP because their goal was to decorate each house with one hundred rolls! Now you understand. It was harmless fun and an easy win to say "yes." People like wins. Families need to learn to give them away freely—cheer, laugh, have fun, and enjoy life. I love Solomon's advice, and it's one of Terry's life verses:

> So I commend the enjoyment of life, because there is nothing better for a person under the sun than to eat and drink and be glad. Then joy will accompany them in their toil all the days of the life God has given them under the sun. (Ecclesiastes 8:15)

Coach

Everyone likes cheerleaders. They are fun, happy, full of energy, and always smiling. As mentioned, our homes need to be places with lots of cheering going on. But sometimes it's necessary to put down the pom-poms and grab the whistle. Another vital part of a family dynamic is coaching. There are times when you cannot cheer people into greatness; you need to coach them. Coaching is the fine balance of telling people what they don't want to hear in a way that they will accept it, with the goal of helping them be what they want to be. In families there are times we all need a little coaching. There are times when the only way to help people change and grow to be more like Christ is to graciously speak the truth in love. Paul writes,

> Instead, speaking the truth in love, we will grow to become in every respect the mature body of him who is the head, that is, Christ. (Ephesians 4:15)

This always works best when our families have invested much energy in building deep relationships.

The only way to accomplish these deep relationships is slowly and lovingly over time. To quote the famous line from "The Tortoise and the Hare," "Slow and steady wins the race." Time builds trust. Trust is essential when you have to blow the whistle to do some coaching. When trust is in place, the coach's words will be viewed as loving and not hurtful. The reason we started with cheering and why it is important is because it balances the coaching. Paul reminds us that all coaching and no cheering will exasperate our children. I think it is safe to say that this truth applies to both parents, not just fathers:

> Fathers, do not exasperate your children; instead, bring them up in the training and instruction of the Lord. (Ephesians 6:4)

Terry and I have had to do our share of coaching over the years. All parents do. Parenting is not for sissies, that is for sure. We have prayed and coached our girls through things like dating relationships, finances, friendships, entertainment choices, college selections, career decisions, and marriage partners. Great job girls on selecting Caleb and Brad. Well done! Life is a series of choices, and some of them are big. Your kids will need help. They will need a wiser, older, seasoned voice at times. Don't be afraid to blow the whistle, call time out, and work through a plan. They may resist at times, but it's still necessary. Remember the investment in building deep relationships that we talked about earlier? This is where that investment pays off. And how about a word of encouragement? The older your kids get, the smarter you will become in their eyes. This makes coaching much more enjoyable. Hang in there!

Challenger

I am a teacher by trade, so I fully understand the impact of a red pen when grading papers. No one likes to see their paper marked up with the red pen; no one! Then, if at the top of the page circled in red is a big fat "F," that is really not a good day.

Here is the truth about families. People sometimes fail. There are times when we simply don't pass the test, whatever that day's test may be. Wives fail. Husbands fail. Kids fail. It's a realistic part of "our" family. So when something or someone goes off the rails, it's important that the red pen gets dusted off and put into play—dusted off because it should be used sparingly. Then when it is used it needs to make a statement. It needs to drive home a point.

God uses times of failure to help us learn all kinds of important biblical lessons and life lessons: humility, forgiveness, grace, mercy, love, and consequences, just to name a few. Peter's challenge as to why we need to continue to grow in Christ fits here perfectly.

> For this very reason, make every effort to add to your faith

> goodness; and to goodness, knowledge; and to knowledge, self-control; and to self-control, perseverance; and to perseverance, godliness; and to godliness, mutual affection; and to mutual affection, love. For if you possess these qualities in increasing measure, they will keep you from being ineffective and unproductive in your knowledge of our Lord Jesus Christ. (2 Peter 1:5–8)

I don't believe any of our families have a mission statement that includes the words ineffective and unproductive. In fact, I believe we desire the exact opposite. For our families to be effective and productive, we sometimes need to persevere through the red-pen moments in order to hold our families to the high standards of following Christ.

We mentioned the sons of Eli earlier in this chapter. Eli was the high priest, and his sons assisted him in presenting the sacrifices of the people before the Lord. Eli was well aware that his sons, Hophni and Phinehas, were violating God's sacred commands. Instead of choosing to dust off the red pen and deal with the issues, he enabled them to continue in their sin.

> Why, then, do all of you despise my sacrifices and offerings that I require at the place of worship? You have honored your sons more than me, by making yourselves fat with the best part of all of the offerings of my people Israel. Therefore, this is the declaration of the Lord, the God of Israel: "I did say that your family and your forefather's family would walk before me forever. But now," this is the Lord's declaration,

> "no longer! For those who honor me I will honor, but those who despise me will be disgraced." (1 Samuel 2:29–30)

What a tragic ending. I often wonder if it would have turned out differently if the leader of the home would have lovingly challenged his boys with truth. The Word of God has included that story for a reason. I pray that we learn the hard lessons from others so we do not have to learn them for ourselves.

Comforter

Sometimes our families need to grab the pom-poms, sometimes the whistle, other times the red pen. There is one last thing our families need to have readily available: the first-aid kit. It's amazing how much a small Band-Aid, with a little tender-loving care, can soothe a painful hurt. Our family has to be the first-aid kit for each other. Our homes must be a safe place and a place of comfort. When the dodgeball game of life beats a family member down, there must be a safe haven to which they can run. We never dare run out of tender-loving care. When a family member foolishly makes a poor decision and is dealing with the consequences of their self-inflicted wounds, family needs to be there. I am reminded of what Paul said to the church in Corinth regarding a wayward church family member:

> If anyone has caused grief, he has not so much grieved me as he has grieved all of you to some extent—not to put it too severely. The punishment inflicted on him by the majority is sufficient. Now instead, you ought to forgive and comfort him, so that he will not be overwhelmed by excessive sorrow. I urge you, therefore, to reaffirm your love for him. (2 Corinthians 2:5–8)

That is the responsibility of a church family as well as a biological family. Family is family. We exercise love in all situations, and when there is godly sorrow, there needs to be a first-aid station close at hand.

Terry enjoys watching YouTube clips of wild-animal encounters in Africa. Of course he always wants to show them to me. So, I watch with my eyes squinted and ready to close in the event that things get a little too "food-chain-ish," if you know what I mean. He is especially fond of the clips that show herds of water buffalo being stalked by a pride of lions. Inevitably, the lions select one poor buffalo and eventually take him down. Then, when it appears all hope is lost, the rest of the buffalo herd comes marching back like an invading army, rescues their family member, and pushes the pride back into the bush. They have figured out that there is safety in numbers. In the end there is a happily ever after. Just had to throw that in. Our families need to take on that same herd mentality. We need to be there for one another.

Our families—each one is a unique bunch. We serve in a unique way. We live in unique circumstances. Some say we live in a fishbowl. Others say we live under a microscope. It really doesn't matter; we are family, and that is what matters. Our family has been chosen by God to be in ministry. That makes us a dodgeball team. At times there are different members within our family that are the underdog on the team. They need the team to rally around them. They are looking for, and longing for, the rest of the team to step up. We must not let them down. May God help us to never abandon the team. We desperately need each other.

The Questions to Wrestle

1. Why do you think God included family failures in His Word? Does this encourage you? If so, how?
2. Rank yourself on each of the four areas mentioned: cheerleader, coach, challenger, and comforter. Which area are you strongest and which area needs the most work, and why?
   (1 strongest, 2 strong, 3 just okay, 4 weakest)
3. Cheerleader. How open are you to saying "yes" to your children when it comes to parenting? Is it more natural to you to say yes or no, and why?
4. Coach. How important is relationship building prior to a coaching moment with your children? Share a couple of ways you have found success in building relationships with your children.
5. Challenger. How dusty is your red pen? Do you use it too much or not enough? What kind of failures are worthy of the red-pen moments?
6. Comforter. Would your children say your home is a place of safety and comfort? Share some ways we can display this to our children.
7. Have you talked to your children about the unique pressures they feel as a pastor's kid? If no, why? If yes, what did they say?

CONCLUSION

I (Kelly) am honored that you made it to the end of this book. You know me a lot better now than you did when we started this journey together. You have heard my passions, my hurts, flaws, and my loves. Thank you for allowing me to share honestly.

How do we wrap this up and put a bow on it? Let's head back to God's Word and our Proverbs 31 wife of a leader. She was a team player. She was a valuable asset to those around her. She was focused. She made a difference. People were counting on her, and she came through. What was her foundation? What are the final conclusions we are to make about this woman? Once again, we find that all-important answer from our Bibles:

> Her children rise up and call her blessed; her husband also praises her: "Many women have done noble deeds, but you surpass them all!" Charm is deceptive and beauty is fleeting, but a woman who fears the Lord will be praised. (Proverbs 31:28–30)

Okay, here is my question when I read Proverbs 31. Do I have to attempt to measure up to this woman's standards? I mean seriously. She sets the bar really high. She seems to be almost perfect. Was she? Is that the point of this passage? Is that our takeaway?

Thankfully, the answer to those questions is a big, fat *no*! Praise God the standard is not perfection. How miserable would life be if every day were measured by living a flawless life? You see, we know for certainty that this woman was not perfect. God's Word is clear. There is no such person among humanity:

> If we claim we have not sinned, we make him out to be a liar and his word is not in us. (1 John 1:10)

No, the standard is not perfection. Can I get a hallelujah!? The standard, however, is fearing the Lord. How about one more moment of open transparency as we end? Will there be days I doubt "HIS calling" on our lives and ministry? Probably. Will there be moments I fail in "my assignment" as a leader and live in sinful behaviors that make wrong influences and drive bad outcomes? Yep. Will there be times I disappoint my husband and instead of bringing him good and not harm, I get them in reverse order? For sure. Will I fail to live up to "their expectations" as a pastor's wife? Without a doubt. Will I sometimes rush into "his battles" and play the role of armor bearer by swinging my favorite sword of sarcasm? Yes, and on occasion I may even enjoy it for a moment. Will I have times of dealing with "our discouragements" that will result in me not filling my L.U.N.G.S. with needed oxygen? More often than I want to admit. Will I disappoint "our family" by coming up short as a cheerleader, coach, challenger, or comforter? Potentially daily.

Here is the good news. None of those things will ultimately stop me from my pursuit of being a woman who fears the Lord. The goal is not perfection but progressive sanctification. Keep striving. Don't quit. Stay the course.

Sometimes you hear a great phrase in a strange place. A while back I talked Terry into doing a twenty-one-day Beach Body workout with me, twenty-one days of pure torture every morning at 7:00 a.m. It sounded like a good idea at the time. Seriously, I had forgotten I even had muscles in some of those areas of my body. But truthfully, in the end it really was painful but good. On one of the workout videos, the instructor made this comment, "Don't let your past define you; let it guide you." I doubt the emphasis was meant to be a biblical one, but it actually is. God never intends for our past to derail us but to help us learn and grow. Here is a great way to look at our past:

> For everything that was written in the past was written to teach us, so that through the endurance taught in the Scriptures and the encouragement they provide we might have hope. (Romans 15:4)

Much of what is written "in the past" of the Bible is a record of failures of both people and nations. It's written to remind us that failures are inevitable but not final, and that with Christ we have the encouragement of His mercy, grace, and forgiveness. Our past does not have to define us, but it can guide us. Paul gave us his amazing testimony in this statement,

> Not that I have already obtained all this, or have already arrived at my goal, but I press on to take hold of that for which Christ Jesus took hold of me. Brothers and sisters, I do not consider myself yet to have taken hold of it. But one thing I do: Forgetting what is behind and straining toward what is ahead, I press on toward the goal to win the prize for which God has called me heavenward in Christ Jesus. (Philippians 3:12–14)

"Forgetting what is behind and straining toward what is ahead." Now, that is a great goal. We can do this! We need to do this; and we can, one day at a time.

Praise God for middle school gym class and dodge-ball day! I'm sure all of the stories and analogies probably stirred up some foggy memories deep in the recesses of your mind. I trust the recall wasn't too painful. I hope you were able to conjure up a few of the exciting victories. In the end, it was just a game. It was middle school, a fading memory at best. So why use dodgeball? Why this illustration? The goal was to use a common-life experience to creatively help us think through life and ministry. I pray it worked. I pray the conclusions drawn have provided a measure of encouragement to you as a pastor's wife. Ours is a unique calling. It takes much prayer, patience, and perseverance. So, let me say goodbye with this prayer for you, your family, and your ministry.

> The Lord bless you and keep you; the Lord make his face shine on you

> and be gracious to you; the Lord turn his face toward you and give you peace. (Numbers 6:24–26)

If you a desire to go a little deeper in working through the ins and outs of being a leader's wife, please check out our ministry, Small Church USA. We have a specific course dedicated to pastors' wives. I would love to connect with you and continue to do this journey together.

Please find us at our website:
www.smallchurchusa.com.

Questions to Wrestle

1. What areas of this book challenged you the most?
2. What are a couple of "next steps" for you in continuing this growth journey as a pastor's wife?
3. What additional topics would you like Small Church USA to address in regard to pastor's wives? Please list them and then email them to Kelly@smallchurchusa.com.

SMALL CHURCH USA

Terry and Kelly founded *Small Church* USA to help guide pastors, pastors' wives and churches to revitalized health. God began preparing their hearts for this ministry, when in 1998 he led them to Crawfordsville, Indiana, a midwestern community of 15,000 people. Upon arriving in small town America, Terry became the lead pastor of an unhealthy, dying church of 20 people. Over the next 22 years as the church got healthy, God accomplished more than anyone could have asked or imagined, and the church grew to over 1,000 people in Sunday morning worship.

Over the years many pastors and churches reached out to learn about their revitalization strategy and success. To meet the many requests, Small Church USA was founded with the goal of exponentially helping pastors, pastors' wives and churches with encouragement and hope. According to the US Census Bureau, 91% of all the communities in the United States of America have a population of 15,000 people or less. These small communities are filled with churches looking for an organization that can relate to their specific context. *Small Church* USA is that organization.

Here are the engagements they offer:

Healthy Pastor

- 6 month participation engagement
- Personal leadership development
- Utilization of a nationally renowned leadership profile
- Limiting cohorts to 4-6 pastors per cohort

Healthy Pastors' Wives

- 5 month participation engagement
- A diagnosis of the five key areas for keeping pastor's wives healthy
- Group size is not limited

Healthy Church Revitalization

- 12 month participation engagement for pastors
- Identifying and diagnosing the five vital organs of a healthy church
- Limiting cohorts to 4-6 pastors per cohort

For more information, please visit our website at smallchurchusa.com or contact us at:
Terry@smallchurchusa.com or
Kelly@smallchurchusa.com

Made in the USA
Las Vegas, NV
03 July 2021

25877822R00083